GW00673463

I can't believe my life has come to this!

How to understand and overcome your fears, move beyond dysfunction, and realize your life's dreams

Dr. Gary Penn

Inner Space Publications
P O Box 491851
Los Angeles, California 90049

ISBN-10 0-615-34861-0
ISBN-13 978-0-615-34861-2
Copyright information available upon request.

v. 1.01
First Edition, 2012
Printed on acid-free paper.

For Jeannine and Cristen

Contents

Introduction

- Does it seem as if you go on making the same mistakes over and over?

- Is your mind mired in fear because you're convinced that your hopes and ideas are doomed to failure?

- Can you clearly identify your personal problems, but you find it difficult to move toward lasting solutions?

- Are you drinking, eating, or smoking too much?

- Have you been overweight or just out of shape for years?

- How long have you been promising yourself that you would change jobs or careers, go back to school, or start a new business?

- How about the people in your life? Do you have the same arguments with your family, friends, or lover every few days or weeks?

- Have your important relationships remained antagonistic or unfulfillng, without the circumstances or feelings improving substantially over time?

- Do you repeatedly pick the wrong people to date?

- Have your human contacts with others faded away

because the Internet is dominating your time and attention?

—〜〜—

So many disappointments, so much positive change that *could* take place . . . yet your life seems to be remaining frustratingly the same. Every day, you go to work at a job that drains the life out of you, and then you come home to relationships that often leave you intellectually, emotionally, and physically wanting more. However much you may have achieved in terms of wealth, possessions, position, and prestige, you still feel frustrated.

And time seems to be doing its best to remind you that there's only so much sand left in the hourglass. The struggles and obstacles we face can begin to feel relentless. The older you get, the more quickly time flies by—whether you're a recent college graduate, a newlywed, a new parent, or someone who sees only deeper lines and graying hair when you look in the mirror.

The demons you struggle with—hate, arrogance, fear of failure, humiliation, shame, anxiety, and depression—continue to dominate the human condition as they did hundreds or even thousands of years ago. Certainly we've become smarter in many ways. Technology has become a juggernaut that's both idealized and feared. It seems as if every month a new invention is unveiled that would have been unimaginable just a few years earlier. As a result, life becomes easier, but also more complex. And although our productivity makes quantum leaps forward, our emotional and psychological health remain stagnant.

You're making the decision to read this book at this moment because you're searching for a new way of being. You're hoping to find a way out of your dysfunctional, repetitious behaviors . . . a way to live the way you know you should be living instead of remaining mired in a psychological prison made up of intrusive thoughts and self-defeating behaviors.

Maybe your impetus to start this journey is a response to your being faced with difficult circumstances. You may be feeling that things can't continue on as they have—that something needs to change. The greatest lessons often carry come at the greatest price: a divorce, a lost job, a drunk-driving arrest. Facing the reality that the life you're living is wanting has brought you to this book.

When tough circumstances or challenging situations arise, you can choose to become crushed, bitter, depressed, panicked, vengeful, hopeless, and full of rage. You can shake your fists at the gods and curse them for dealing you such a dreadful hand.

You can crawl inside your defense mechanisms and hide behind a damaged personality and an invented identity. You can blame circumstances and other people for your lot in life. These are the sometimes-easy or familiar options and the ones you're likely to choose in moments of weakness or when you're unaware. But, in fact, what they really do is give you a false sense of comfort and protection from truths that you're unable or simply unwilling to face.

There Is Another Option . . .

- You can *choose* to not become a victim of circumstances, whether those circumstances include a horrible upbringing, a tragic incident, or a dreadful series of events.

- You can *choose* to pay attention to that voice at the back of your consciousness that keeping telling you that something's desperately wrong and that things can and must change.

- You can *choose* to understand how your psychology impacts how you live, and then you can commit to making real and lasting changes.

This option is far more challenging, at least in the short run, but over the course of your lifetime, it can be tremendously rewarding.

This better option is what this book is about. It's about questioning why you're the way you are and about getting answers and techniques what will help you climb your way out of your dysfunction. When you develop these insights, you'll be able to begin the journey of challenging the psychological underpinnings that have repeatedly thrown you into dysfunction.

Awareness is half the battle. The other half is actually changing your behaviors. Self-awareness will propel you to live an ever-expanding, ever-challenging, ever-invigorating, actualized life—a tall order, but also a worthy goal. More precisely, self-awareness is a process. Evolution is not an end-game dynamic. It's is a process of continual growth, a path, a journey. And the feeling of hope that brought you to this book is an important step in this process.

Through this book, you'll be compelled to evolve, and once you get started you'll never want to stop. As the old saying goes, "Give a pair of leather shoes to a man who's been wearing wooden ones all his life, and he'll never go back to wooden shoes again."

I promise you that if you have the courage to start this journey, you'll never want to go back to living in the (false) comfort of your familiar dysfunctions because:

You can change.
You can live a life of psychological,
physical, and emotional health.

This I know. This is what I've experienced in my own life and have seen with the many people I've had the honor to work with over the years. This is why I wrote this book.

Gary Penn, PhD
Los Angeles CA
2012

> *At the end of each chapter, I've included some "Take a Moment" exercises. These are a way to help you look at your life and how you may be unconsciously arranging it for failure, dysfunction, and underachievement. They also point you to ways to change.*

chapter 1

WHY?

(...do we love our defenses?)

A few years ago, I was staying at a resort in Puerto Rico. On my first morning there, I went to the restaurant to have breakfast. Seated at the next table was a married couple. The woman was very attractive and slender. The man was a very different story. He was about six feet tall, must have weighed at least three hundred pounds, and was completely out of shape.

An elaborate buffet had been laid out, and the couple went over to serve themselves. When I saw what the man brought back to their table, my jaw dropped. His plate was overflowing with layers of greasy, fattening foods—a huge helping of fried fish, a dozen pieces of bacon, at least a half-dozen sausages, many spoonfuls of scrambled eggs, a giant helping of fried potatoes, two bagels slathered with butter and cream cheese, and a corn muffin dripping with more butter. I watched in fascination as he rolled up his sleeves and proceeded to devour every last crumb. He then proceeded to make another trip to the buffet, this time returning with a plate piled high with pastries, cakes ... and three low-fat yogurts!

It was awe-inspiring to think about the mental gymnastics he must have performed in order to allow himself such gluttony. When he had taken his shower that morning, he must have seen his body as he stood in front of the mirror. There was no way he could have overlooked the layers of fat and excess skin hanging from his stomach and breasts. As he climbed the steps to the restaurant, he surely felt the strain on his muscles and heart caused by all the extra weight he was carrying. He had to know that his horrible eating habits and the obesity it led to weren't just bad for his health but were truly dangerous. It wouldn't have surprised me if that man was taking medications for hypertension, diabetes, or a host of other conditions related directly to his weight. But even with reality screaming at him that restraint was necessary, his damaged psychology still made him allow himself to devour enough food for a family of four.

"Why?"

No doubt this is the question so many of us face. After all, here you are, opening another self-help book because you want to try to improve your life. Why do you have to go through this? Why is life so difficult to figure out?

You say you want to be happy, and yet you avoid making the (seemingly simple) changes that will help you achieve contentment. You know what the guidelines are. You know that self-awareness, introspection, integrity, discipline, and a commitment to physical, intellectual, and emotional growth are among the qualities that lead toward happiness.

It doesn't take a great deal of insight to realize that watching five hours of television a day, eating an entire bag of peanut butter cups, or drinking a daily bottle of vodka isn't in your best interests. Why, then, do you keep on doing these things?

Why do people say they want to be happy—but then keep on doing things that bring them so much misery? It's the easiest thing in the world for us to see how *other* people screw up. You watch others fall again and again and you roll your eyes and wonder, "Why don't they ever seem to learn? Why can't they see how obviously counterproductive their actions are?"

—⁓—

Take Rick, for example. "He's always late!" his friends commiserate. "It's constantly getting him in trouble. *Why* doesn't he simply give himself an extra half-hour?"

But it never seems to happen. Rick's been late his whole life, and it's affected his relationships with his friends, his family, and his coworkers. It's also cost him numerous jobs. In spite of all the negative feedback he gets from the world, though, he stubbornly refuses to take personal responsibility and always insists that the real culprit are traffic, or a last-minute phone call, or lost keys, or . . .

Then there's Cheryl, whose friends can't understand why she keeps going from one loser to another. "Can't she see that she's heading for heartache yet again?" they wonder. "Even though there are nice guys who want to date her, she keeps choosing jerks!"

Once again, their comments sound reasonable, but Cheryl's record with men continues to be pathetic. She's beautiful, intelligent, and accomplished, and is constantly meeting caring, successful, affectionate men who would love to date her. But she insists that it was just her "rotten luck" that her last four boyfriends were less than stellar, to put it mildly. She's convinced that she had no way of knowing in advance what everyone around her could clearly see—that the men she dates have two things in common: they drink too much, and they have little or no ambition.

Zach, on the other hand, is the king of underachievement. His bewildered friends shake their heads and ask each other: "Why does Zach always dumb himself down? He's so smart, but he keeps taking jobs he could do with his eyes closed."

Highly educated and extremely bright, Zach repeatedly accepts jobs that not only pay far too little but also bore him to tears. Haunted by his failures, he laments that he "coulda been a contender." He attributes his lack of success to bad luck, misplaced trust, competitive coworkers and management, and a dearth of opportunity. His intelligence, impressive though it is, isn't enough to help him see that good opportunities are always landing on his doorstep. So we have to ask ourselves: why can't Rick comprehend how much giving himself those extra few many minutes to "relax" before he gets ready to leave is costing him? Why does everyone but Cheryl realize that the new guy she's dating is yet another loser? Why doesn't Zach see what's right in front of him?

In other words, why do we run headfirst into dysfunction? Why can't we learn, grow and evolve? After a series of bad relationships, shouldn't the next person you give your heart to be someone who won't beat you up, cheat on you, or be emotionally unavailable? After years of drudgery working at a repetitive, uninteresting job, it stands to reason that you would finally try your hand at something that fulfilled you emotionally, intellectually, and financially. At some point it may be time to finally take a stand for real change.

The world is full of broken people whose optimism has been destroyed by regret and despair. Personal tragedy isn't defined only by obvious catastrophes like death, divorce, or financial ruin. Sometimes it can be seen in the constant hum of unfulfilled dreams, lonely nights, and self-loathing.

It can be heard in the anguished voice within our minds that keeps shouting at us in the words of the title of this book:

"I can't believe my life has come to this!"

—⁘—

You can see this dynamic every day and all around you. All you have to do is pay attention. Do any of these people remind you of yourself?

- The office worker who drives an hour to work each day only to spend eight more hours perform-

ing tedious, boring, unchallenging, and unfulfilling
tasks

- The actor who, at age forty, is still waiting tables
  and hoping that his "big break" is just around the
  corner

- The woman who sits at home alone night after
  night while her husband goes out drinking with
  friends

- The man who languishes in solitude, desperately
  lonely but unable to connect with another person

What's so perplexing is that, even though you're unhappy,
your actions suggest that you prefer the status quo (however
miserable you say it is) traveling the road that will lead to lasting change. It's a common misperception to believe that real
change requires a herculean effort and that, even then, there's
no guarantee of success. Given the "facts" as you see them, the
concept of "change" can become so daunting that you often
give up before you ever start.

Instead of using your insight and intelligence to better yourself, you may actually use these assets to keep things exactly as
they are. You'll use drugs, alcohol, and food to medicate yourself
and to lessen the pain that goes along with living the (unfulfilled)
life that you've so carefully crafted. You'll submerge yourself in
work, food, sex, or media consumption . . . you'll do whatever it
takes just so you can get through the day without setting about
the hard work that can bring about true, lasting change.

But you're left with a paradox—on one hand, you say you
want to a live happy, fulfilling, creative, passionate, and complete
life, but on the other, you engage in behaviors that consistently
lead you toward an unhappy, unfulfilled, uncreative, and pas-
sionless existence.

It can seem that as if you're living with a self-destruct button labeled "Screw up my life, and screw it up good!" and that you can't but continually pushing it. Eventually you can become expert at rationalizing why you keep on pushing this button. Rationalizations are essentially "happy drugs" for the psyche. You plead your cases before an inner judge, but the judge is on the take, has a predetermined conclusion, and subtly convinces you to continue on with your "easy" (i.e., dysfunctional) behavior(s).

In the case of the insatiable Puerto Rican diner, his emotional psychology no doubt led him to the stance of, "I want to eat *what* I want and *as much* as I want," and his internal "judge" ultimately condoned his gluttonous behavior. Maybe his internal (or perhaps unconscious) arguments sounded like this: "Since I'm on vacation, calories don't really count.... I've worked like a dog for the past six months, so I deserve a little splurge.... My wife loves me the way I am, so why change if she doesn't mind? ...I made up for all these calories by climbing the stairs up to the restaurant...."

The problem with rationalizations is that they work! You're debating with yourself and presenting yourself with the outcome that you really want to move toward. Rationalizations can make practically any dysfunctional behavior palatable. How else can you explain the crazy things that people do?

Take the case of a married man who "convinces" himself that it's okay to have sex with a prostitute by telling himself that he's really not doing anything wrong since his actress-wife recently had a love scene with a handsome actor. He asks himself, "Don't I deserve pleasure from another person as well? Besides, isn't oral sex almost the same thing as masturbation?" Then he rationalizes that his actions weren't so bad because he didn't have feelings for the prostitute.

Why do you allow this kind of distorted logic to convince you that it's okay to engage in behaviors that are obviously destructive? Because underneath your public or personal protestations, you really *want* to engage in them, and you don't want to suffer the painful feelings of deprivation that you would experience if you abstained from them.

> **The fact is, you're actually striving to keep in place the very things you say you hate about yourself because rationalizations allow you to continue to engage in these behaviors while maintaining a sense of inner integrity.**

Another trick we use to maintain the status quo is to deflect or avoid blame. You break out this tactic when you feel trapped and can't bring yourself to admit an error. How many times have you endured severe emotional tumult because you couldn't admit you were (get ready for the dreaded word) . . . *wrong?*

In a heated argument, you could have owned up to your lapse in judgment or lack of consideration by saying something like:"Boy, did I screw up! I can see that I was acting selfishly and that I was incredibly inconsiderate of your feelings. I need to work harder on being more considerate of what you're feeling."

This sounds sounds pretty mature, doesn't it? And if you had said these things, they probably would've been well received, the conflict would probably have de-escalated, and everything would have worked out well. Nonetheless, the only time you allow yourself to make such an admission is *after* you've tried every possible way not to have to. You'll commit to hours or even days of intense conflict in an attempt to deflect any responsibility. Eventually, only emotional exhaustion will compel you to give in and acknowledge your mistakes.

Minor confrontations often turn into major conflicts. Small, insignificant flare-ups morph into all-out wars. Before you know what hit you, things have escalated to a point where you're lobbing personal attacks in an effort to protect yourself and deflect blame. Do these examples sound familiar?

- "What do you mean, I don't listen to you? That's all I do is listen! Maybe if you'd stop nagging me all the time, I'd pay more attention!"

- "So I didn't call you when I said I was going to! You're so needy sometimes!"

- "I can't believe you're mad just because I want to go over to Mickey's house to watch the game! It's not my fault that you don't have any friends!"

The original issue (not paying attention, not making contact, going out solo too often) is soon forgotten or is seen as unimportant compared to the hurtful retorts you use in your counterattacks. In the heat of battle, nothing becomes more important than protecting yourself from blame—not integrity, not advancement in your career, not the hurt feelings of the people you love.

Once again, all of this begs the question of "Why?" If you know you're wrong, why don't you just admit it? The people you're arguing with know you're wrong—after all, they're screaming it at you!—yet on you fight. For what? You know you're wrong, yet you feel compelled to defend and attack, attack and defend. You stampede onward, compelled to self-destruct and to pull apart the personal and professional relationships whom you say you love and value. Because in essence you're saying, "I'm willing to risk destroying this incredibly important relationship just so I don't have to admit that I'm wrong."

This kind of defensive posture can affect all of your relationships. It'll prevent you from being able to really hear your critiques from your boss. Instead of listening carefully to what he or she has to say, your defensiveness will compel you to employ a variety of counterattacks. You'll discount the messenger ("She's an idiot!") or come up with excuses for why you failed ("I'm overworked ... I was sick last week ... I never received the software I was supposed to get ... "). You'll cling to your rationalizations no matter what the cost.

Why We Cling to Rationalizations

At first glance, it's relatively easy to label people who continually move toward these types of behaviors as psychologically "sick," while a psychologically healthy individual can be defined as someone who moves towards functionality and self-affirming behaviors. On closer inspection, however, the demarcation between "self-destructive" and "self-affirming" may not be quite so clear. Why? Because from the perspective of people who engage in these (seemingly) dysfunctional behaviors, their actions reflect their best attempt to achieve personal happiness and self-actualization.

But ... however miserable your life may appear, and no matter how bleak things may seem, as of this day and in this moment, the life you're living represents the best you can do. As of this moment—sitting in your room reading this book, having the friends and relationships you do, having your work, your hobbies, and your vices—the life you're living *as of this moment* represents you trying with all of your will and resources to be happy. This conclusion is self-evident, because *if* you truly knew another way to live your life, and *if* you believed that this new lifestyle would make you happier, and *if* you felt capable of doing what was necessary in order to follow that path, *you would most certainly do it.*

> *Wherever you are in your life—*
> *whether you're an alcoholic or married to one,*
> *mired in a job you hate, desperately lonely,*
> *hitting someone or getting hit—*
> *and no matter how difficult things may be . . .*
> *as of this moment, this is the best you can do.*

No doubt the above statement seems absurd when look at our actual behaviors. How in the world is underachieving in your career, marrying people who physically or emotionally abuse you, drinking until you pass out, or lying for no apparent reason be the result of a quest for "personal fulfillment"? How can staying in an abusive relationship be a "personal best"? How does smoking marijuana three times a day or popping painkillers represent a "best attempt" at life?

Frank is a perfect example of these contradictions. He's madly in love with his wife, yet he continues to have extramarital affairs. Look at all the hoops he needs to jump through in order to have these affairs:

- He has to constantly be covering his tracks.

- He has to be vigilant about not leaving any clues such as phone calls, receipts, and the scent of the other woman's perfume.

- He has to repress his feelings of guilt and shame.

- He spends beyond his means on hotels, dinners, and gifts.

- He runs the risks of making the other woman pregnant or of contracting sexually transmitted diseases.

- He loses time with his two children, whom he loves very much.

♦ Most important, he puts his marriage in jeopardy.

After every encounter he feels guilty and remorseful. He promises himself, "This is the last time," yet whatever will-power he claims to possess melts as soon as another attractive woman comes into his sights. If his infidelities threaten to destroy what he says he values more than anything else—his marriage and his family—how can it be considered a "win" for Frank to continue to engage in them?

Well, it depends on which "Frank" we examine. For example:

- **"Fear of intimacy" Frank:** This Frank is terrified of giving himself fully to any one person. His affairs provide emotional cover, which makes him feel less emotionally vulnerable.

- **"Anger toward women" Frank:** This Frank has a great deal of unresolved anger toward women that stems from his relationship with his controlling mother. Cheating serves as his way of dealing indirectly with his misogyny so he doesn't risk taking out these feelings directly on his wife.

- **"Fear of confrontation" Frank:** This Frank has never learned to express his anger directly. He feels dominated by his wife and is unable to stand up to her. Instead of confronting her directly, he retaliates against her indirectly through his affairs.

- **"Low self-esteem" Frank:** This Frank is convinced that sooner or later his wife will cheat on him, so he reasons that it's better to carry out a "preemptive strike" by being unfaithful first.

So, when we see more deeply into Frank's nature, what seem-ed irrational at first glance now seems a little less so.

From Frank's (unconscious) point of view, having sex with different women feels safer than having to confront the psychological issues that tug at the core of his being.

- Maybe if your father hadn't labeled you a "loser," you wouldn't drink. But getting drunk is better than staying sober and thinking of yourself as colossal failure.

- Maybe if your self-esteem wasn't distorted because your mother made it obvious that she favored your brother over you, you would break up with your cheating spouse. But if you're convinced that no one else would have you, of course you'll put up with infidelity.

- Perhaps if your parents hadn't ignored you for days at a time whenever you upset them, you would leave your physically abusive husband. But for you isolation is worse than getting slapped in the face because at least that slap proves that someone is taking you into account. You continue taking the abuse—in fact, you'll go on seeking it out—because without it you feel alone and worthless.

"Why?" is the crucial question you have to ask yourself and keep asking yourself because if you're able to become truly aware of all the underlying psychological processes that propel you to engage in dysfunctional behaviors, you stand a fighting chance of bettering yourself.

Once you discover how you got to be the person you currently are, you can begin to confront these dynamics directly instead of having them lurking around in your unconscious mind like undersea monsters that will keep dragging you back under into dysfunction. In other words:

> **Either you deal with your issues—**
> **or they'll deal with you.**

In the following chapters, we'll explore the psychological dynamics that have been keeping you flailing around in the quicksand of your life. It isn't that you're stupid or masochistic. It isn't that you *like* the pain that's interfering with your life and happiness. The deeper truth, though, is that you're actually thankful that things aren't worse—even though you may not be clear about what *"worse"* really means. The truth is that you're terrified of what's under and beyond the obvious pain and dysfunction that you're so used to. That's what's scaring the daylights out of you, because stopping your dysfunctional behaviors will lead to your true self being exposed, and this can be very scary.

Like the Wizard in *The Wizard of Oz*, you're screaming at everyone (including yourself) to "pay no attention" to the man behind the curtain. You're spending every last ounce of your strength trying to hide away . . . far, far away. You're hoping to present yourself as "the Great and Powerful Oz," not as the scared, vulnerable human that you're terrified to expose. How sad . . . and how very unnecessary!

—∿—

However, the goal of this book is to help you understand how you got where you are, and then to give you the tools that will make it possible for you to live the life you so desperately want.

> **It is possible to be happy.**
> **It is possible to achieve self-actualization.**
> **You can make this a reality!**

take a moment...

1. Identify one or more behaviors or habits that hinder your growth.

2. See if you can identify the rationalizations you use to allow these behaviors to exist or continue. For example, here's a rationalization that someone might employ to continue to smoke marijuana: "Smoking weed is fine. I'm not hurting anyone, and it relaxes me."

3. Can you identify what you gain that encourages you to engage in these behaviors? Try to go more deeply, beyond the obvious gains that seem acceptable (for example, "Marijuana calms me down") and to get to the deeper ones that aren't so obvious ("It numbs my feelings and makes the time pass more easily").

Can you believe
what I just did?!

Have you ever wondered why the game of "Peekaboo!" brings such joy to infants? It doesn't seem as if it should be such a big deal, yet infants are always thrilled every time they cover and uncover their face. It seems as though they never tire of this game. Once they get the hang of how the game works, they marvel at the fact that you're still there when they cover and then uncover their eyes. When they take their hands away and see you still standing in front of them, they're filled with anticipation and bursting with excitement. The psychological dynamics that underlie this seemingly simple activity can help you to understand the formation and maintenance of your self-concept and self-esteem.

Newborns are just that—newly born. When babies open their eyes and look out at the world, they don't have the experience or knowledge to realize all the work and effort it took to create their environment. Everything just is. Everything revolves around them because they haven't yet developed the perspective to imagine other persons as separate, self-aware beings. In the world of babies, magical thinking—not physics or scientific facts—rules. Babies don't comprehend that someone built the couch they're lying on, or that the light in the room is the result of electricity, lamps, and bulbs.

Babies don't know how the people in front of them got there, where their clothes came from, or why they're playing with them. In the minds of babies, *they* are responsible for the creation of everything they experience, as attested to by the fact of its very existence in their world. Infants have not achieved "object permanence." For them, when an object isn't visible, it no longer exists. The reason why "Peekaboo" is such a charge for infants is that every time they play the game, they believe that when they uncover their eyes, *they* are creating us, and that when they cover their eyes and make us "disappear," they are destroying us. So their laughter and glee can be interpreted as something like, "Holy cow! Look what I just did!"

It's this sense of omnipotence that serves as the underpinning of the psychological structure that ultimately defines your sense of self. Young children are certain of their influence in being the causal force in creating their world—whatever happens in their world is a result of their own personal power. This dynamic affects children's self-concept because, from the child's perspective, "Good things happen because *I'm* good, and bad things happen because *I'm* bad."

The experiences of cute little four-year-old Katie describe how this dynamic can affect a child's psychology. As she's carrying a plate of spaghetti from the kitchen to the dinner table, she trips and spills her food all over the floor.

"You stupid idiot!" her mom screams. "You can't do *anything* right!"

The psychological process by which Katie internalizes her mother's diatribe is significant. Being only four years of age, in her mind she's the creator of her world, so she thinks (and feels), "Mom's responding to me, and I'm responsible for her screaming at me. She's only responding to the stupidity and idiocy that exist inside me."

Katie's too young to have the ability to understand that her mother's angry and out of control, and that the reason she's this way has nothing to do with Katie or with the fact that Katie dropped her food. Katie hasn't reached the developmental stage where she can look at the situation objectively, from a perspective that will be available to her as an adult. Like all children at her age, she's self-absorbed. She's trying to find out who she is and how the world (which from her perspective is completely centered around her) responds to her. Unfortunately, in this case, she's learning an awful lesson.

An additional aspect of Katie's taking responsibility for her mother's hysterics is that, even though she may *feel* omnipotent, she also realizes that she needs her mother to provide a safe, caring, and loving environment for her. After all, she's only four. If she were to truly believe that her mother was a hysterical, out-of-control woman, her world would feel entirely unsafe. Where could she go? What could she do? She couldn't call a friend. She couldn't get on her Big Wheel, pedal to the nearest hotel, check in, and order a peanut butter and jelly sandwich to be sent to her room!

Katie depends on her parents for her entire existence. Imagine how terrifying it must be to depend completely on someone when that someone is angry and irrational—not a pleasant thought or reality. This is where Katie's omnipotence rescues her, because instead of feeling that she's at the mercy of an irrational mother, she takes comfort in the belief that (according to her omnipotence) she herself is the one who has created all this upset. This type of mental gymnastics instantly rehabilitates her mother, who goes back to being kind, giving, safe, and loving—and who's vicious only because of *Katie's* awfulness. To four-year-old Katie, this is a win. Her omnipotence allows her to sleep peacefully because, when she lays her head on her pillow that night, she can let herself believe that tomorrow her mother will treat her better—if only Katie can make herself worthy.

Does this type of altered perception sound familiar? When another person treats you poorly, do you take responsibility and ask yourself: "What did *I* do to make him scream at me that way?" or "She said she'd call me back. Something must be wrong with *me* to make her break her promise?"

Of course, the psychological impact on Katie would have been diametrically different if her mother had been kind, generous, patient, understanding, and loving. In that case, when Katie was carrying her plate of food and tripped and spilled it all over the floor, her mom would have responded by saying: "That's okay, sweetie. Accidents happen. Let's get this cleaned up and make you another plate."

Katie would have understood her mother's kindness and lovingness to mean: "Mom's responding to *me* . . . Mom's being sweet and kind and loving because (in keeping with Katie's omnipotence) that's who I am. I'm a good girl. I'm worthy of love and respect, and that's why I receive it."

When you were young, your parents were gods. They gave you life. They kept you safe. They explained the world to you. You believed what they told you. You may still be following a particular religion or registering a particular political affiliation because, decades ago, your parents told you that was right. While I'm certain that many of you love your beliefs and have found your own meanings and truths within them, the point I'm making is that a great many of the values that you hold—and the ways that you see yourself—are beliefs, thoughts, and feelings that you accepted without question because they stem from the psychological "concrete" that your parents laid into your consciousness many years ago.

I certainly don't mean to simplify the human experience. I don't ascribe to the belief that we're all blank slates when we come into the world and that our environment is one hundred percent responsible for our personality. I believe that each of us is born with a stamp that says "This Is *Me*." Some may believe that this is a function of neurons or physiology, while others lean toward the influence of the soul or experiences from previous lives. Whatever the cause may be, each of us seems to have certain idiosyncratic personality traits. Nevertheless, the experiences you had when omnipotence dominated your worldview are, in large part, responsible for the psychological "concrete" that forms the bedrock of your present sense of self.

Having an experience like the one described in the first "Katie" scenario can leave you with an indelible stain of psychological ugliness. You'll go through life struggling to an attempt to cure an unshakable, depressing sadness. The constant hum of damaged self-esteem will drive you to do whatever you can and to be whatever's required so that one day you can hear the sweet song of what you're convinced will be your salvation: "My dear daughter (or son), you're the best! I can't tell you how proud of you I am and how much I love you. I know that as a parent I made serious mistakes. You never did anything to deserve them, and I'm sorry from the depths of my soul. You're wonderful, and the fact that I didn't have the presence of mind and heart to tell and show you that is my fault, not yours."

When we've had a difficult childhood, our desire to hear these words can become incredibly powerful. It is these words, or words like them, that you can spend a lifetime seeking, because without them, you feel trapped in psychological purgatory—a purgatory that was created by the very people you're presently looking to for the cure.

Your sense of self may have been constructed from false "truths" that were cemented into your psyche by way of your childhood omnipotence—"truths" that you'll spend your lifetime running from, all the while unable to realize that you're running from your own shadow.

No matter where you go or what you do, these "shadow selves" remain dark reflections of your inner shame. In an attempt to be paroled from your psychological hell, you'll try to prove to your jailers that you've changed (you're never going to drop that plate of spaghetti again) and are now deserving of their unconditional love.

What's unfortunate is that you're seeking to be healed by people who remain incapable of or unwilling to help. Your attempt to heal yourself entails seeking a cure from people (Mom, Dad, caregivers, and so forth) who invariably end up injecting you with more of the same psychological venom that made you sick in the first place—truly an ingenious (albeit ludicrous) solution!

You're being driven by unconscious demons. Your unconscious, empowered by a sense of childlike omnipotence, relentlessly plays a personal theme song that echoes your flaws, which caused such harshness. Over a lifetime, this dynamic can lead you to continue running from your shame and toward the possibility of healing, only to find yourself in the hands of other persons who continue to disappoint you and inflict yet more pain on you.

And this fascinating, agonizing process began long ago . . . with a simple game of Peekaboo.

take a moment...

1. Think back to a traumatic experience that happened in your childhood (for example, a divorce, death, betrayal, molestation, humiliation, etc.). Describe how you conceptualized this experience at the time. (Note: Try not to get into your head, so to speak. In other words, avoid simply reciting the logical, emotionless version of what happened. Instead, write down how you felt personally responsible for what happened, and how that made you feel.)

2. It's common for us to be concerned about what others think of us. What do you imagine people think of you when they first meet you? (For example, "They think I'm great, smart, funny, stupid, boring, annoying, ugly, a burden . . .")

take a moment...

3. If someone does something inconsiderate to you such as missing a lunch date, breaking plans at the last minute or talking to you in a condescending or disrespectful manner, do you automatically feel as if you did something wrong or that you deserve it?

   a. If your answer is "Yes," can you trace back to when this type of reaction first took root in your psyche?

   b. Can you identify any benefits that you may believe you get by taking responsibility for the feelings of others?

chapter 3

I just want

somebody to love!

Omnipotence-generated feelings are exceptionally difficult to shake because they course through our entire psyche. In my therapy practice, I work with some of the kindest, most compassionate, loving, and decent people—who remain convinced that they're nothing but a burden to those around them. As I discussed in the previous chapter, in an attempt to alleviate their pain, they seek approval from the very people who heaped criticism and disapproval on them or who withheld love from them:

- "Even though I love photography, Dad always wanted me to be a doctor. If I become one, perhaps he'll finally think I'm somebody."

- "My parents will disown me if I don't marry a Jewish man. I love Clark madly, but I'm going to have to break up with him. I just don't have any other choice."

The hell you put yourself through!

This dynamic remains in play with other relationships as well when you find yourself attracted to parental "stand-ins." You'll marry them, work for them, and become friends with them. Whether they want it or know it, you imbue these surrogates with the essence of your early caregivers in the (unconscious) hope that they'll be able to see that you're worthy of their unconditional love.

On the surface, this seems silly. Would you ask someone who's deaf to judge whether you can sing well? If your father was too busy to spend time with you, shouldn't you make sure that the person you marry would make you a top priority? If your mother was hypercritical, wouldn't you naturally be attracted to people who are supportive, encouraging, and who admire you? Unfortunately, the answer is no. Counterintuitive though it sounds, you're going to be attracted to people who possess the same shortcomings as those who created the toxic environment you grew up with in the first place!

This may make you feel either idiotic or masochistic. It's absurd to choose to associate with people who continue the cycle of emotional pain, yet this is exactly what happens. Why else do Sheila's boyfriends always turn out to be alcoholics? Why else does John tolerate such a dependent, clingy wife? If Maggie's so into success, why does she hang around with such losers? If J.R. wants a committed relationship, why does he always seem to get involved with married women?

Once again we're back to "Why?" Why doesn't logic reign? If you could never please Dad because you always felt like a failure around him, shouldn't you find someone who approves of and encourages you now that you're an adult? Of course! Why then did you marry a belittling, micromanaging, emasculating woman? The answer to this simple question reveals the elegance and ingenuity of the unconscious.

Suppose I'm sick and in desperate need of medical attention. I drive to the local hospital, where I'm given my choice of physicians. In this hospital, each doctor speaks a different language. One speaks English, another speaks Spanish, another Armenian, another Chinese, and so forth. If the only language I speak is English, and there are no translators available, I'll obviously choose the English-speaking doctor because I want to make sure that I'm understood and that my doctor is someone that I can relate to and understand.

In the same vein, we all seek out people who, metaphorically, speak the same language we do.

For example, Brian has a horrible self-image, due in large part to his years of having been subjected to his father's emotional absence and his mother's constant criticisms. If you ask him what type of woman he wants to date, he'll honestly say that he wants someone who's kind, supportive, available, and present—someone who sees his intelligence, heart, and soul.

He begins dating two women simultaneously. Julie thinks he's just great. She finds him attractive, intelligent, funny, kind, and compassionate. She treats him with respect and wants to spend as much time with him as possible. But . . . even though these are qualities that Brian *says* he wants and honestly *believes* he wants in a woman, he just can't seem to connect with Julie. A true connection is elusive because the "docking bay" in his psychology that would allow him to fully accept her praise and affection is missing. Not only is he unable to connect with her, he also (unconsciously) mistrusts her. Why? Because his unconscious is whispering, "She must have a screw loose to think so highly of you! She must be lying, or maybe she's out to set you up for a big fall. The message he receives is "Stay away!"—and eventually he obeys.

On the other hand, Stephanie, the other woman he's dating, has nothing but complaints about him. She tells him that he doesn't have enough ambition and that he should work out more often. She disparages his career choice and states that he should do something that carries the promise of more money. He disappoints her constantly, and she lets him know it. And even though Brian says that these behaviors are exactly what he doesn't want in a woman, he's *very* attracted to and comfortable with her. Why? Brian feels understood on a very deep level because Stephanie treats him in a way that connects with his fundamental beliefs about who he is. She truly understands him, and he trusts what she says, even (or rather, especially) when it's hurtful.

Another example of this dynamic is revealed in people who can't accept compliments. When told that they look good, they immediately put themselves down: "You've got to be kidding! I look terrible!" or "You think this rag looks good? I don't think I could sell it at a garage sale!" These people repel praise but have psychological Velcro when it comes to criticism.

Cindy is a beautiful and intelligent woman. At twenty-five, she could easily adorn the cover of a magazine. Nonetheless, she's convinced that she's ugly and stupid. She obsesses that her arms are too fat and her breasts are too big, and that she isn't smart. Rarely do we have a therapy session when she doesn't complain about some physical or mental deformity.

It wasn't difficult to trace the beginnings of her self-loathing. She grew up in a harsh fundamentalist Christian household where any expression of self-pride was considered a sin for which she would be condemned to hell. In addition, her father was a hateful, critical man who constantly told her that she was fat and unattractive. This God/father combo left her feeling psychologically deformed despite her physical beauty, and her skewed self-image has defined her adult relationships. At a conscious level, she wants someone who will accept and love her for who she is, yet her unconscious directs her to connect with people who do exactly the opposite—because she automatically devalues people who think highly of her. If a man tells her that she's smart, she sees him as stupid because only an idiot would think she has any brains. She thinks that men who find her beautiful are lecherous, superficial, and sinful. When all is said and done, the only kind of man she really trusts is one who sees her the way she sees herself, which mimics the way her father treated her. Unsurprisingly, she's attracted to men who are critical, insecure, and misogynistic.

Cindy and Brian are living their lives by Groucho Marx's

famous quip: "I refuse to join any club that would have me as a member." When you feel worthless and then someone treats you in a way that speaks to this feeling, you actually feel understood because you're psychologically wired to accept such a relationship. You'll forgive your friends when they don't invite you to their party or when they break plans at the last minute. Not only do you forgive them—you also (secretly and unconsciously) respect them for treating you badly.

Connecting the Dots, Seeing the Patterns

One of the benefits of getting older is that you begin to see patterns emerge. You may have had bad luck once or even twice in relationships, but when you see that the same type of person keeps entering your life over and over and over, you can be assured that ghosts from your past are exerting their influence.

It's not a coincidence that you find yourself repeatedly attracted to the same type of person. In order to break out of this pattern, you need to start connecting the dots. You need to become introspective and to try to understand your own role in creating your world. When all is said and done, it's important for you to realize that on some level it's *your fault*, and not bad luck, when you find yourself in relationships with angry, violent, flirtatious, seductive, cheating, or emotionally cut-off mates. This doesn't excuse their bad behavior, but it does imply that you're responsible for the choices you make.

Here's an analogy: suppose that my boyhood bedroom was a few yards from a railroad track and that every so often a train would come by and make a tremendous racket. As an adult, I come upon an apartment that's inexpensive because it overlooks a busy freeway. While most people would immediately reject such an apartment, I find the noise soothing.

Juanita provides an excellent example of this dynamic. She grew up with a physically and emotionally violent father who screamed at and hit her. Now she's an adult and on her first date with Henry. When they arrive at the restaurant, the host tells them that their table won't be ready for another twenty minutes. Henry proceeds to cause a big scene by yelling at the host and the restaurant manager. Most women would be so appalled by such behavior that there certainly wouldn't be a second date. Not Juanita. She isn't appalled in the least. Henry's behavior doesn't seem odd or inappropriate (at least he didn't punch the manager!). In fact, she may feel protected (either consciously or unconsciously) because she interprets his behavior as his standing up for himself and not allowing himself to be taken advantage of. To Juanita, Henry's behavior feels like mac'n'cheese—psychological comfort food. And from this point on, it's relatively easy to see how this relationship will progress.

You can't fix a problem that you don't acknowledge exists, but the more you take responsibility for the choices you make, and the more you refrain from blaming your situation on bad luck or on being duped by a convincing partner, the better you'll be able to create a life that mirrors your conscious dreams.

Identifying the problem is the first step, and the techniques I'll be outlining in this book will help you find a new and healthy way of living—one based not on fear and despair, but rather on maturity, clarity, and optimism.

take a moment...

1. Look back over your past few romantic relationships. Do you see any common themes among them?

2. If you do see recurring patterns, see if you can connect them to earlier experiences in your life.

3. What internal beliefs about yourself have allowed you to become involved with people who with hindsight you realize that you shouldn't have?

chapter 4 It's not true is it?

When I was twelve, my father invited me to join him to a roundtable discussion at the temple that we belonged to. There were about twenty men sitting in a circle, with me the only adolescent among them. World events were discussed, and ideas were flying around the circle. Everyone was passionate and eloquent . . . I was enthralled!

As the discussion progressed, a thought came to me that I believed was smart, pertinent, and important to the discussion. I really wanted to contribute, but since they were all shouting their opinions and, because I was only twelve, it was difficult to find an opening.

Finally there was a lull in the conversation and I had my chance! My heart was beating out of my chest and my adrenaline was pumping. I was terrified and excited at the same time.

Now was my moment to be included . . . to shine . . . to show that I was smart and thoughtful . . . to be part of the group. I got two words out: "I think— "

Immediately my father turned to me and in a voice that everyone was able to hear said, "Shut up! This is for adults! You sit there and listen!" Mortified, shamed, and humiliated, I slowly looked around at the group members. Many averted their gaze. Others looked at me with pity and what I imagined to be disgust. I looked down at the floor and used all the resources I possessed not to cry. The humiliation was huge. I wanted to run away and hide in a place so secluded that I would never have to face those people again.

Even though this happened decades ago, feelings of shame still wash over me as I write this. What was especially insidious about what happened was how I viewed this event. I felt humiliated. I felt as if something was wrong with me. I felt small and worthless. As a twelve-year-old, I didn't have either the psychological strength or the perspective to really understand what happened, and it took years before I was able to sort things out in a way that reflected reality. That reality revealed that my father was an angry, competitive, insecure, and sadistic person—tremendously flawed as a man and as a parent —and that what happened that day had everything to do with him and nothing to do with me.

These types of events become embedded in us like timeless monoliths—psychological "Stonehenges" that can reconfigure our psychological makeup and exert a dark influence on our psychology for years to come. They tell us of times when we were (more accurately, when we *felt*) worthless, stupid, despicable, and flawed. And we go on believing that these characteristics are somehow indicative of who we are today.

Our defenses are tasked to protect us from further psychic damage. They do whatever's necessary to make sure that we never again have to face the kind of pain that we experienced when we were small and at the mercy of flawed parents, predatory adults, cruel classmates and acquaintances, and any other people who may have left a lasting impact on us.

If you believe that you're defective, it'll be difficult for you to try new projects or relationships or challenging jobs. You *know* you'll fail since you're using the corrupted information that was seared into your psychology years ago. Based on your past experiences and traumas, you're certain that you'll get hurt (or humiliated, as I was when I tried to speak up at the roundtable discussion). Understandably, you'll avoid trying anything risky in any realm—personal, business, or otherwise.

When these types of damaged self-perceptions get frozen

in time, something that was seen as true a long time ago has little validity in today's circumstances—if examined with today's eyes. These types of historical fears inform you that the world is indeed flat and held up by a tortoise, and that sailing on a ship will lead to your demise. Even though present-day facts tell you that the Earth is round and that millions of people have sailed around the globe, your psychology, frozen in time long past, remains unconvinced. It refuses to accept a new reality and convinces you to stay safely on shore.

This is maddeningly frustrating because *intellectually* you know that today's circumstances are different from when you were young and defenseless. The adult version of you realizes that you no longer need to protect yourself and tells you:

- "Ask her out already! She knows you like her! What's the worst that can happen?"

- "You know you've been wanting to open a restaurant for years now. What harm can come from taking a single class to learn more about it?"

But unfortunately, the old psychic warriors of your past still hold sway. And those fears make simple tasks, such as writing a business proposal or asking someone out to dinner, *feel* as if you're being asked to defuse a bomb—disconnect the wrong wire, and the consequences will be catastrophic.

When irrational fears hijack your intellect, you end up talking yourself out of taking relatively easy, incremental steps. When catastrophic thinking reigns, fears mushroom and anticipated consequences are seen as potentially disastrous. Eventually these fears become an inescapable prison . . . a receptacle of your missed opportunities and forgotten dreams.

Becoming conscious of your feelings is the best method for you to challenge and ultimately conquer your fears. It may seem that you're drowning in a sea of personal incompetence and forthcoming ridicule, but a rational examination of the real facts will make you realize that you're only in three feet of water. All you have to do is get your legs under you and stand up.

When Billy was seven, his father divorced his mother and moved to another city. As most (omnipotent-thinking) children do, Billy blamed himself (both consciously and unconsciously) for his father's exodus. As I discussed earlier, taking on the responsibility for his father's absence allowed Billy to maintain an image of his father as good and loving, which was critical for a small, defenseless boy to believe. Unfortunately, this mental manipulation carried with it severe consequences.

Dad's exit seared into Billy's consciousness the core beliefs that "I'm a bad boy" and "I make people leave." To him, these beliefs were absolute truths and were unaffected by logical and rational thinking (which were unavailable to him as a little boy). These ideas became the bedrock of a protective (and often unconscious) wall where they remained diligently on duty.

Because these types of believes are buried in a psychological "cryogenic chamber," they feelings don't change as we age. A house may undergo remodeling and additional construction, but the foundation remains unchanged. As Billy grew older, his belief that he made the people he loved leave eventually became generalized to people at large.

Billy's damaged psyche psychology, armed with the mission of protecting him from getting hurt again, reasoned that isolation is the safest alternative: "If I don't get close to people, they won't get to learn how awful I am." The fact that Billy has grown up into a kind, caring, intelligent person who has a great deal to offer and who is accepted and loved by many people does not override this unconscious core belief. Past ultimately trumps present.

Breaking Through to the Ugly Voices Within

If you can bring yourself to break through your defenses, you may find that untold numbers of ugly beliefs and feelings are lurking:

- "I'm a failure and I'll always be a failure."

- "I'm ugly."

- "I'm stupid."

- "I make people leave me."

- "I'm a burden."

- "I'm not as good as my brother or sister."

- "I caused my parents' divorce."

- "Mom drank because she had to put up with me."

- "My mother's life was ruined because she had to take care of me."

No wonder it's more comfortable to stay on the surface of your psychology. You're facing the enemy, and it's you. Compared to having to face your true thoughts and feelings, psychological oblivion and a defensive stance count as wins. In fact, you may jump through extremely high hoops to keep them from ever being exposed.

People who know about what happened, and certainly people who witnessed it, would have a more accurate view of what happened in our past ("Your father left because he couldn't get along with your mother, and he didn't visit you because he had problems with intimacy. It wasn't your fault. You were just a sweet little boy. What could you possibly have done that would have been terrible enough to make him leave?").

Sounds logical, doesn't it? In fact, it makes perfect sense. In regard to your past, what *could* you have done that was so bad?

But even though your adult, rational self knows this, you just can't seem to integrate this truth into how you see yourself and how you live your life.

One fundamental aspect of mental and emotional health is the ability to acknowledge and work through these archeological myths. An excellent way to do this is to engage in a thoughtful analysis of the "I" that makes up of our sense of self. This process can be tremendously helpful in gaining a deeper understanding of your sense of self.

This process of self-exploration will allow you to correct your faulty self-perceptions. You'll benefit by exploring the foundational underpinnings of your self-concepts with fresh eyes and by challenging the present-day thoughts, feelings, and behaviors that stem from them. The goal is to consciously create new self-perceptions, ones that are no longer based on the defective person you believed yourself to be but on the person you've become.

take a moment...

1. Write down some emotionally traumatic events that happened to you when you were growing up.

   a. How have these events affected the way you see yourself now?

   b. List the differences between how you continue to believe yourself to be and the person you have actually become as an adult. (For example, "I still feel as if no one will ever love me, although, as an adult, I'm surrounded by people who actively love me.")

_____

_____

_____

_____

_____

_____

_____

_____

_____

_____

_____

_____

_____

_____

5 Can you see
the real me?

To recap: in your early developmental years, your core personality constructs became hardwired into your psychological "mainframe," and these constructs continue to influence you today. A generally positive and nurturing environment will most likely have allowed you to feel a basic sense of inner safety. This means that you actually like your own company and that you're confident that you can draw upon your inner resources to succeed.

An overall negative childhood experience, on the other hand, can lead to low self-esteem. When you're saddled with low self-esteem, you may try to compensate for your (perceived) flaws by trying to get others to think well of you. It's a common coping strategy to adopt a secret and often unconscious agenda in your interactions with other people so they'll ultimately think well of you. Regardless of circumstances, or your mood or internal feelings, it becomes imperative that you present yourself as someone who's nice, caring, sweet, and accessible. What's ironic is that ultimately this is manipulative and selfish behavior because your interactions invariably become about *you*. When all is said and done, requiring that others leave with positive impressions of and reactions to you makes authentic experience impossible.

In the service of creating these positive impressions, you end up creating a false persona because you end up swallowing your anger, disappointments, or personal desires that you may feel are at odds with the desires of others. While this strategy may prove effective in the moment, you will often lose yourself in the process. Very often people will like you, but they may not respect you—because the price you pay for *acting* nice, never getting angry, and avoiding conflict is a low-grade depression since you're depressing so many of your genuine feelings.

What's so sad is that your natural good nature is instantly changed the moment you *try* to be something. I believe that I'm smart, but if I *try to appear* smart, the interactions that I have with people will be markedly different. Trying to appear smart will most likely leave me appearing pompous and arrogant. By not trying and by just being, I can relax into my interactions with others. For example, instead of pretending that I understand the meaning of a word, I can easily ask for the other person to define it. Presenting myself as a human *being*, rather than as a human *"trying,"* allows me to feel comfortable in the moment, regardless of how I might be perceived by my audience.

In addition, a damaged self-esteem can lead you to define yourself in "either/or" terms. You're either smart *or* stupid, caring *or* uncaring, nice *or* mean. This type of either/or thinking convinces you that you need to *act* a certain way ... because if you don't *try* to be smart, caring, or nice, your true self will be exposed. Behind this anxiety lies the nagging question, "What type of person would be exposed if I stopped 'trying'?"

On the other hand, when you own your true self you can present yourself to the world in a relaxed, honest way without hidden agendas. For example, I consider myself to be a nice person, but I'm not always nice. I'm a considerate person, but I'm sometimes selfish. I'm a smart person, but sometimes I'm incredibly dim. Monitor your self-assessments, and when you do, work diligently to *not* define yourself by the last thing you've done, said, or felt.

> *Just because you're not being nice*
> *doesn't mean that you're being mean.*
> *Just because you're taking care of your needs*
> *doesn't mean that you're a selfish person.*
> *Just because you're angry*
> *doesn't mean that you're hateful.*

For example, one way you can determine whether or not your fear of being "mean" is based on a sense of present-time reality or instead is a feeling that's attached to a damaged sense of self is to try to imagine what a truly "mean" statement would sound like. Say it out loud and then compare that statement to thoughts and feelings that you're afraid would be interpreted as mean if you expressed them. My guess is the two statements will be very different.

The need to have others think well of you can overwhelm your intrinsic self—the self that's truly you, that's as smart as you are, as honest as you are, as capable as you are. Instead of being free with your thoughts and feelings, you'll do your best to anticipate what you imagine will make other people think well of you—and in this process, you'll end up muting your opinions and downplaying your successes.

You may justify a false persona by convincing yourself that you enjoy pleasing people. After all, what's so bad about wanting other people to think well of you? The answer, of course, is that there's nothing wrong with pleasing others, but it's important that you examine the cost that comes with *having* to please others.

When I see patients like this, I visualize that they're sitting in front of a huge bookcase stacked with volume upon volume of thick books, and that every page in every book is blank. I imagine that these pages contain everything that these people ever thought or wanted to say throughout their life—

but didn't. None of their dynamism, passion, humor, disappointment, anger, and rage was ever written on the pages of their lives. Why? So they could present a version of themselves that they hoped others would like.

Unfortunately, this defense can work exceptionally well. People end up genuinely liking you. They like the "showroom" edition. The problem is that *you* know the real truth. It would be like my wearing a toupee to cover my baldness so I'll look handsomer. Even if my toupee worked perfectly and women told me how sexy and handsome I was because of my beautiful hair, I would still feel unsexy. I would feel like an unattractive man who was able to fool people. But imagine how I'd feel if I were to present myself exactly as I was—sans toupee—and women still found me attractive!

You need to move to a place of being ... being in the moment and learning to be comfortable being a flawed person ... a flawed person but a real person ... a person who has spectacular qualities as well as ones that need to be improved upon. I consider myself an evolving being. My personal motto is that I try to be a little better today than I was yesterday and a little better tomorrow than I am today. Certainly I'm flawed, but I'm also trying. My growth requires that I see my flaws without hating myself for having them. If I can see them with peace and clarity, I can begin to try to understand them and improve myself.

Stop *trying* so much. Just be ... be in the moment and present yourself to the world as you are ... a flawed person who's working toward getting a little better every day. In return, you'll find yourself *living* a more authentic life, *being* a more authentic self, and *attracting* more "real" people.

take a moment...

1. What psychological toupee do you wear to cover up your "flaws"?

2. What is the supposed "truth" that you feel this toupee is trying to cover up?

3. Can you identify how and when this supposed "truth" was created in your psyche? In other words, who placed it there, or what event(s) caused it?

chapter 6

Have
a burger on a bun

When I go to McDonald's, I get a hamburger, fries, and a drink. What's great about McDonald's is that I know exactly what to expect: a meal that's inexpensive, quick, and filling. The experience is exceptionally consistent. I can go to any McDonald's in the world, and I'd never be disappointed. I've never tasted a McDonald's hamburger and fries and said, "What the heck is this? This tastes strange!" Quite the contrary. It's pretty much the same food whether I go to a McDonald's in Los Angeles, Miami, or Tokyo. I don't go there too often because of health reasons, but, once in a while, it's just what I need and want.

On the other hand, supposing I'm craving a fresh lobster dinner with all the trimmings. If I went to McDonald's expecting such a meal, I'd be very disappointed. In the same vein, many of us make this same type of mistake when it comes to relationships. Even though you know that certain people in your life are the equivalent of a burger and fries, you approach them hoping for lobster—and when what you ultimately get is the burger, you feel disappointed, confused, angry, and discouraged.

To continue the analogy, the "Golden Arches," the drive-through, and a hundred other clues are screaming out that there's no lobster to be had, yet you repeatedly make the mistake of thinking that if you ask in just the right way, a five-course lobster dinner will be waiting for you when you drive up to the window!

Paul's Story

Paul spent his entire life seeking lobster from his burger-and fries father. Although his father was a critical, competitive, and withholding man, Paul kept looking for unconditional love and validation even though his father never him gave any indication that he was capable of giving these things, or was willing to do so.

It didn't matter that Paul was bright, successful, and popular. His father treated him the same way he always had, with criticism, a lack of interest, and a lack of caring. Whenever Paul had contact with his father, he would fall into a type of psychological wormhole. The years would melt away and he would psychologically become younger and younger. All the maturity and success he achieved seemed to evaporate. Under his father's critical gaze, accomplishments that Paul had every right to be proud of—graduating college with honors, a screenplay that had been bought by a studio, a loving marriage—lost their importance.

Nevertheless, Paul remained intent on winning his father's unconditional love and approval. The irony of winning unconditional approval eluded Paul . . . not on an intellectual level (it's pretty easy to see the contradiction), but on an emotional one.

Every father-son encounter became a test. For example, something as simple as leaving a phone message took on tremendous importance. When Paul's father called back in a timely fashion, Paul felt elated. On the other hand, when his father didn't call back, or called back hours or days later (which happened most often), Paul felt disheartened. He felt responsible for his father's response (or lack thereof), and he was left with the feeling that he couldn't interest his father in even making a simple phone call.

A vicious circle developed. The more Paul went to his father for approval but failed to receive it, the worse he felt—

and the worse he felt, the more he needed his father to throw him a lifeline.

I believed that Paul's escape from this dysfunctional emotional loop hinged on whether or not he could accept an extremely difficult truth that for decades his father had been communicating (nonverbally) to him … a truth that was crystal clear yet emotionally devastating: "Dad doesn't and never will care about me in a healthy way. And if he does have positive feelings, he's unwilling or unable to express them."

Accepting this type of truth, especially about a parent, is difficult, to say the least. It's the adult version of telling a child that there's no Santa Claus. Paul diligently, and consciously, resisted accepting this truth. Even though he had every reason to believe the exact opposite, Paul stubbornly clung to the hope that if he could only learn how to ask in just the right way, a feast awaited.

Truly accepting his father's emotional limitations would mean that Paul would have to give up seeing his father as someone who had the power to grant him the psychological salvation that he so desperately craved. His acceptance of this "new" reality would mean letting go of the dream of finally hearing his father tell him, "Paul, you're a wonderful son. I love and admire you. You're such an incredible person—smart, kind, loving. I must have been blind for not seeing it until now. You've made me very proud."

I understood that letting go of this dream would be difficult in the short term, but I was also convinced that accepting the relationship as it was and not as Paul wanted it to be would free him from disappointment and self-doubt.

In relationships, it can be very stressful when one person achieves personal growth while the other person remains stagnant. One good example of this dynamic is the happily married obese couple who are uncritical and accepting of each other. One day, however, the wife becomes sick and tired of her body and decides to do something about it. She drastically changes her eating habits, goes to the gym four times a week, and hires a personal trainer. Because of her dedication and diligence, she finds that eighteen months later she weighs one hundred and forty pounds. Her husband, on the other hand, has done nothing of the sort. He has continued to eat as much as he ever did and to live his comfortable, sedentary life. Given the divergent paths the two of them have taken, you can imagine the strain this dynamic could put on their relationship.

It's very common for relationships to disintegrate when one partner decides to change his or her dysfunctional feelings, thoughts, and behaviors while the other partner stands pat. Things that were once acceptable are now questioned and challenged. For example, a woman begins therapy and develops the courage to speak her feelings. She goes home and informs her husband that it's unacceptable for him to continue having tête-a-tête dinners with his ex-girlfriend once a month. Her edict throws a wrench into their "peaceful" (yet depressing) relationship.

What if the husband enjoys having dinner with his ex? Since his wife had never objected before, he might say, with more than a little frustration, "That therapist you're seeing is nothing but a troublemaker."

In the same vein, a husband may decide that he doesn't want to go on putting up with his wife's constant criticisms. In so doing, he's demanding that *she* learn to relate to *him* in a different way. But what if she isn't ready to change, or doesn't know how to communicate with him differently? Becoming more aware of one's true needs and feelings often strains relationships.

Therapy became Paul's psychological "fitness training." As he grew more psychologically fit, he began to think, feel, and behave differently. One example of this was exhibited in the weekly phone calls he made to his father. He would make these calls even though he felt that he was bothering his father, who rarely sounded as if he was glad that Paul had called. His father would answer Paul's questions with one- or two-word replies, and he rarely inquired about what was happening with Paul. After the call was over, Paul invariably felt exactly as he used to when he was a little boy—insecure, worthless, and full of self-doubt.

During one session, I asked Paul how long he thought it would take for his father to reach out if Paul decided to stop being the one who initiated the weekly calls. Paul estimated six months. This was a profound statement, yet it didn't seem to carry any emotional charge because it reflected the normal state of their relationship. Also, Paul was thinking only in theoretical terms; that is, he never really thought that he would go through with not calling his father anymore. As long as he could maintain the illusion of a positive father-son relationship, all was well. Calling his father every week was his way of keeping the illusion intact. The truth, however, was waiting to be found, if only he would allow himself to see it.

My goal was to help Paul see the relationship exactly as it *was*, not as he imagined it was or hoped it could be. I therefore suggested that Paul refrain from initiating his weekly calls and then sit back and see what would happen. My goal was to reveal a truth that I believed would set Paul free from his self-doubt, free from his constantly asking himself, "*Why* the withholding? *Why* the rejection?" In short, free from blaming himself for not receiving something that was never available to be given to him in the first place.

Paul decided to follow my suggestion and stopped his calls. Week upon week and then and month upon month came and went without his father reaching out. During those months, Paul worked very hard in therapy. He began to look at his father and their relationship in a new way. After processing a great deal of anger, bewilderment, grief, and sadness, Paul was able to accept his father for the man he truly was: critical, withholding, unavailable, and emotionally distant . . . a man who was capable of maintaining only superficial relationships, not just with Paul, but with everyone in his life . . . a true "burger-and-fries" man.

Along with this understanding came a sense of peacefulness. No longer was Paul blindsided by disappointment, since his eyes were no longer closed to the truth. He grew to expect only what little the "golden arches" offered, without hoping for more.

Finally, after five long months, his father called—and Paul learned that during this time, his father had also gone through an unexpected change. His father must have realized that something in his son had fundamentally changed. Maybe he missed his son's adoration and neediness but, whatever the reason, he actually started to reach out more, and for the first time in years he actually asked Paul out to dinner!

Thanks to Paul's new insight and behavior, his relationship with his father actually improved.

Accepting Reality for What It Is

You have the ability to accept reality for what it is instead of mentally manipulating it so it's less painful. Suppose you're standing in a room and notice a foul smell. You look down and spot a gigantic pile of dog poop on the floor. The horrible, disgusting smell is a warning: "Stop, look, and stay away!" To take this metaphor further, you may want to ask yourself if you're someone who cleans up the messy reality—or who immediately pulls out a can of air freshener and sprays and sprays until the smell is fully masked.

Once Paul learned to see and accept his father's limitations, he began to look to others for validation, love, and support. He crashed through the defensive illusion that had kept him depressed and insecure, and was able to embrace his world and the people and relationships in it with clarity. He realized that, however comforting, compelling, and enticing as those "golden arches" had been, they had been giving him only a "burger and fries" experience and nothing more. By finally accepting this, he was able to find fulfillment at the many "lobster restaurants" that were open and eager to serve him.

take a moment...

1. Is there someone whose approval you desperately seek? (Note: The person need not be alive. It may be that you hope to achieve something that they would have approved of if they were still around.)

2. What would this person's approval mean to your sense of self?

3. What would this person's disapproval mean to your sense of self?

4. If this person is alive, see if you can list some ways in which you go to extraordinary measures to nurture the relationship, such as not saying what's truly on your mind or always being the one who initiates contact. What do you think would happen if you stopped doing these things?

Why won't

he just listen to me?

We all have reasons for why we do or don't do things that we feel we should or shouldn't do. In fact, we're so committed to these reasons that when close friends and family members identify our flaws, we immediately become defensive and start offering myriad reasons as to why their beliefs of our behaviors are misguided and the suggestions that they're advocating are untenable.

It's important that you monitor your defensive behaviors. Try to notice if you react *instantly*. If you immediately counter whatever suggestions or opinions are given, and if you do this without being reflective or thoughtful, you're leading with your defenses. To be able to consciously consider what advice or criticism you're being offered, it's important for you to give yourself a few moments to consider what's being said from a calm and thoughtful place. Immediate counterarguments are a strong signal that your defenses have been activated. However, when you're able to get beyond your instant counterarguments, you may be surprised at what you find. For example:

> **Friendly advice:** "I really don't think it's a good idea to be meeting men by going to bars."
>
> **Your instant response:** "A lot of nice guys go to bars! I can't believe how arrogant you are!"
>
> **Feelings that may underlie your instant response:** "I'm terrified of being alone. If a guy's really nice, he's not going to want me anyway. The

guys at the bar may not be Prince Charming, but at least they're better than nothing."

—◊—

Friendly advice: "Maybe you shouldn't call in sick again. You called in sick last week to go to the ball game."

Your instant response: "Listen, life is a game. Big deal if I take off. My boss just took a three-week vacation. If he complains, I'll just tell him that he's not the one to talk."

Feelings that may underlie your instant response: "I've got to get mine. No one's going to give me anything. No one looks after me, so I've got to look after myself."

—◊—

Friendly advice: "Spying on your girlfriend is bound to backfire. She's never done anything to make you mistrust her."

Instant response: "If she's not doing anything wrong, what's the big deal if I check up on her?"

Feelings that may underlie your instant response: "I can't believe she truly loves me. I know she's going to leave me anyway. I just don't want her to make a fool of me."

—◊—

Friendly advice: "If he hits you again, leave him. You deserve better! You don't have to put up with such a creep."

Instant response: "He only hits me when he drinks. You don't see the other side of him...how loving he can be."

Feelings that may underlie your instant response: "This is the best I can do. I'm so worthless that I deserve his abuse."

Rationalizations can be very powerful forces. They can make completely dysfunctional behaviors seem like the most rational things in the world. Fortunately, reality demands acknowledgment. A four-hundred-pound man can rationalize the reasons for his excessive weight and why he can't lose it for just so long, but eventually he'll be forced to contend with diabetes, hypertension, bad knees, and other possibly life-threatening health conditions.

Most people decide to change only when reality finally overwhelms their denials and rationalizations—when your spouse files for divorce, when you receive a third DUI, or when you're passed over for promotion once again. These are the existential moments when life refuses to put up with your explanations any longer ... when the world stops going along with the press release that you've been putting out to the world, and to yourself.

Very often you know better than anyone else (therapists included) what behavioral and emotional changes you need to make to solve your problems. Lack of intelligence or insight is rarely the reason for underachievement or dysfunction. The woman who stays with a man who repeatedly cheats on her knows that she should leave him, and the four-hundred-pound man knows it's not a good idea to eat that box of cookies. Think of all the truly brilliant people who live miserable, destructive lives. If people who are morbidly obese truly don't know that eating a box of cookies is bad, then they need more help than simplistic suggestions can offer.

> *Dysfunctional behaviors often mask deep uncomfortable feelings. Your need to hide from uncomfortable feelings is preventing you from doing what your intellect is telling you is good for you.*

One of the primary goals of therapy is to make the unconscious conscious. This can be an incredibly difficult and laborious task because the psychological defenses that are in place are committed to blocking self-exploration. Whenever unconscious material is threatened with exposure, you'll find yourself instantly, and often unconsciously, moving into a defensive position. Before you know it, you'll find yourself acting defensively, without knowing what's driving your behavior.

The way out of this mindless cycle is to bring your unconscious and uncomfortable thoughts and feelings into crosshairs of your conscious awareness, to zero in on them, and to have the courage to look at them unflinchingly. If you succeed, you'll find yourself able to examine your uncomfortable feelings without your defensive psychology automatically defaulting into manipulating reality. With the aid of your adult self—or, as Freud called it, the *observing ego*—you can begin to identify and then deal with your shameful and heretofore unconscious thoughts instead of continuing to allow them to deal with you.

Shining Light on Our Mind-Monsters

Each night when little Mikey goes to bed, he's terrified by the shadow pattern cast by a lamp and a plant in the corner of his room. In the dark, the shadows look like horrible, dangerous monsters, and he hides under his covers, hoping that the monsters won't notice him.

It's only after his mom plugs in a nightlight that he realizes that there aren't any monsters and that what he thought were monsters were nothing more than scary shadows. The light has caused a change in his awareness, and his certainty that there were monsters in his room was conquered immediately.

So it is with your psyche. As long as the light of awareness remains off, the "monsters"—the unpleasant thoughts and feelings—that lurk in the depths of your consciousness are free to wreak havoc. Awareness is the enemy of these mind-monsters. Switch it on, and they can be examined, held up to rational thought, and ultimately defanged.

This may sound simple and easy, but painful thoughts and feelings generate powerful defenses, and these defenses are committed to keeping these thought and feelings (that you're unlovable, stupid, defective, and so forth) undetected. With the specter of such difficult thoughts and feelings lurking deep in your psychology, it's understandable that your lack of awareness isn't really a bad option. Most of us are waging a deep-rooted battle between our need for healthy exposure and our need (or desire) for dysfunctional secrecy. It's a battle of wills. Which will win—your need to protect yourself from these thoughts and feelings, or your push to evolve?

It's as if your uncomfortable feelings are locked away in a chest buried deep in a psychological haunted house, and the mere sight of the haunted house can be so frightening that it will stop you from any internal exploration. What's worse, imagine your horror when you realize that the self-exploration that will save you entails not only going into the haunted house, but also descending into the dark, cavernous basement where this psychological chest is buried—and then unlocking the chest and discovering what lies hidden inside!

It's important to remember that underneath all your bluster, you really are quite vulnerable and fragile. However much you may want help, you may fear that the treatment is going to be worse than the illness.

The way you travel through life can resemble Autopia, the guided car ride at Disneyland. When you're behind the wheel, you may think that you're in control of the car because it responds appropriately when you turn the wheel and step on the gas or the brake. This feeling represents your conscious awareness. Underneath your car, however, is a raised track that puts limits on where it can ultimately go. This track represents your unconscious, and as long as you stay on this track, you'll continue on the same path—and go on making the same mistakes over and over again.

These unconscious "tracks" will ultimately dominate your behavior. If you've been let down by people who were supposed to support and love you, you may find yourself testing people to see if you can trust them. You may unconsciously create drama as a way to test the dedication and depth of caring that others have for you. You tell yourself: "Sure, they love me when things are going well, but let's see how they'll react when I act out." Meanwhile, your unconscious belief is telling you: "If they can love me when I'm acting like such a jerk, then they must really love me."

The Will to Fail

Failing can be an ingenious (though obviously dysfunctional) way of working through unresolved issues. You have total control of this process. No matter how many people tell you to do things differently, if you really want to fail, then fail you will. Unconsciously, your hope is that your failures will serve as retaliation against those who gave you only conditional and not unconditional love: "If you won't love me exactly as I am (as a flawed but valuable person), then the hell with you!"

Your defense mechanisms are very possessive. They were created to defend you, and defend you they will, even if the price is lost jobs, broken relationships, or cirrhosis of the liver. Your defenses have taken an oath of secrecy and any breach is seen as treasonous. Only you know the shame you carry. Only you know the ugly truths that you fear will be exposed.

Your skeletons are staring back at you from the depths of your soul and shouting: "*Never again* will I be hurt, humiliated or shamed!" In response, you'll do whatever's necessary to protect yourself from the pain and humiliation that exposure would bring. But behind your shame and fear lies a self that is waiting to be healed and loved.

> *Many of us fail as a way of saying,*
> *"I'm not going to change who I am*
> *(even if I know would be good for me)*
> *just so you'll love and accept me.*
> *I'm going to prove to you what an awful person*
> *you were and still are by making myself a failure and*
> *'living down' to your low expectations of me."*

take a moment...

1. Sometimes you fail to achieve the success you're capable of. See if you can identify a secondary gain that may have come with your failures. Have you ever avoided or sabotaged success because you knew that it would make the people who had failed you happy? Have you ever felt: "I'll refuse to achieve success because you should have loved me in good times and in bad"? To which people in your life have you directed these "purposeful failures"?

   a. If you could have told that person directly what you hoped your failure would communicate, what would you have said?

take a moment...

b. Describe the fears that prevented you from telling that person what you wanted to communicate. Here are some examples:

"They would leave me."
"They would laugh at me."
"They wouldn't take me seriously."
"They would tell me I was just complaining again."
"I'm never listened to anyway, so why try now?"

_____

_____

_____

_____

_____

_____

_____

_____

_____

_____

_____

_____

_____

_____

_____

_____

8 My defenses
let me down (thank goodness!)

Let's continue exploring the intricacies of our conscious and unconscious fears and the ways in which they impact our lives. There's a direct relationship between how well these feelings are repressed or rationalized and the level of dysfunction they cause. To live an integrated, actualized life, you must uncover these feelings and deal with them directly. The problem that you face is: how can you deal with feelings when you aren't aware that these feelings exist in the first place?

We can work toward uncovering our unconscious in the same way that scientists attempt to find undetectable particles that exist in the universe. Scientists are convinced that undetectable (and therefore theoretical) particles exist. They base this assumption on the effects that these (theoretical) particles have on matter that they *can* detect. If particles that *can't* be detected affect particles that *can* be detected, that confirms the existence of the undetectable particles.

In the same vein, you can become aware of your "invisible" (unconscious) thoughts and feelings by studying the effects they have on your observable thoughts, feelings, and behaviors. The existence of your repressed feelings is confirmed by the trail of your dysfunctional behaviors, thoughts, and feelings, which are like a trail of psychological "breadcrumbs" that can help you to uncover your unconscious.

The book and movie *Contact* exemplify this point. The story focused on a scientist who was trying to contact an extraterrestrial civilization through the use of radio telescopes. After a great deal of time and effort, the radio telescopes detected a signal, in the form of pulse tones, coming from a planet that was circling a star located light-years from Earth. However, detecting the signal was only the first step because the scientist needed to decipher the information that was contained within the pulse tones. A blind colleague who had a highly developed sense of hearing was able to solve the mystery. Because of his acute sense of hearing, he realized that within the easily detectable tones were harmonic subtones, and it turned out that these subtones contained tremendous amounts of information—in this case, blueprints on how to build an extraterrestrial transport vehicle.

Without deeper introspection, you'll continue to respond to your dysfunctional behaviors with platitudes such as: "Life sucks," "I'm a loser," or "I drink because my husband is a jerk." It's only through sustained self-examination that you'll be able to decipher the psychological "harmonics" that these behaviors are trying to communicate to you. Through this process, you'll find that many of your dysfunctional thoughts, feelings, and behaviors contain invaluable clues to your internal world.

Nancy's Fear of Abandonment

Nancy's story is a "slice of life" example of this dynamic:

> **The outcome:** Nancy forgot that she had a lunch date with her husband and instead went to a yoga class with her girlfriend.

> **Nancy's rationalization for the outcome (otherwise known as "life happens"):** "My sister called me in tears. She has a professor at school who hates her. Right after she called, my friend called and asked me if I wanted to take a yoga class with her, and I instantly said yes because I was so wound up."

Harmonic subtones of the outcome (forgetting lunch): "I resent my husband for working so much. He doesn't have time for the kids or for me. Why should I go out of my way for him? We never go out, and we hardly make love anymore. I'm hurt, I'm angry, and I feel rejected."

Deeper harmonic subtones: "If I speak my mind and tell him how I truly feel, I'll be rejected. Whatever I say will be devalued. If I say what I truly feel, those I love will leave me."

Developmental experiences that led to these feelings: Nancy grew up with a depressed and emotionally distant father who was sad, quiet, and dismissive. When she was twelve, she was chosen by her drama teacher to play the lead in her school play. When she came home bursting with excitement, her father responded with a total lack of interest and suggested that she spend more time studying her math homework and less time on "ridiculous hobbies." Crushed, she soon dropped out of drama, never to pursue acting again.

Nancy's mother was difficult as well. She was depressed, self-centered, and jealous of Nancy. Nancy's conversations usually ended up with her mother talking about herself or complaining about something that Nancy had done wrong. Nancy grew up feeling unimportant and convinced that her feelings really didn't matter. She certainly didn't feel safe expressing herself. By digging beneath the obvious outcome—her "forgetting" to meet her husband for lunch—we hit a bedrock of insecurity based on early emotional abandonment. Nancy's true feelings ("No one cares about me because I'm not worth caring about, and if I speak up, the people I love will reject me") were buried in her unconscious, and she unconsciously believed that her husband would treat her with the same lack of interest that she had experienced as a child.

Given the (false) choice of preserving her marriage or speaking her feelings, Nancy chose to forgo the latter. Nevertheless, even though she sentenced her unexpressed feelings of anger, hurt, and insecurity to the "gulag" of her unconscious, they kept demanding her attention. "Forgetting" the lunch date was an elegant way to do this.

All this information was waiting for her to discover it. She had only to look!

Zach's Stalled Career

Remember Zach? Let's examine the case of his stalled career:

> **The outcome:** Zach can't seem to find a job that rises to the level of his abilities. Although he's highly intelligent and possesses many marketable job skills, he's caught in a lifelong pattern of underachievement.
>
> **Zach's rationalization for the outcome:** "I'm pigeonholed. There's no room for advancement, and I'm too old to start over. I've sent out a few resumes, but I haven't received the responses I want, so what's the point in even trying?"
>
> **Harmonic subtones of the outcome (underachieving career):** "I'm terrified to seriously look for a better job. I'm insecure about whether I can actually get one, or whether I'll be able to keep it if I do."
>
> **Deeper harmonic subtones:** "Trying is the first step toward failing. I'm not smart or capable enough. I'll surely fail."

Developmental experiences that led to these feelings: Zach's father was competitive and critical. He always focused on what Zach lacked instead of on his son's many skills and talents. This left Zach with gut-wrenching self-doubt. Deep down, he was afraid that perhaps his father was right and that he never *would* amount to anything.

These feelings, safely tucked away in Zach's unconscious, drove him to avoid any serious attempt to excel, so he focused on goals that were ultimately unattainable. He reminded me of a high jumper who could barely clear six feet but would then set the bar for his next jump at seven-and-a-half feet. When he inevitably failed, he wasn't all that devastated because he knew that he really didn't have a chance to succeed anyway.

In the same way, Zach went from one project to another—always busy and always planning, but never succeeding—an elegant defense. "Trying" satisfied his conscious self, and when he ultimately failed, he actually felt a sense of relief because it proved that his father's criticisms were justified.

Zach was stuck. He wanted to move forward but felt too paralyzed to take action. So there we have it—a stalled career. Closer examination reveals that his rich psychological structure used failure as a means of creating safety—yes, he underachieved, but at least he could fall back on being a man of potential.

Self-Hatred—a Dead End

It's essential that you look at your dysfunctions in a new way instead of instantly beating yourself up for possessing them. It can be tempting to hate yourself for your dysfunctions because, counterintuitive though it may sound, you can use hating yourself as a misguided way of trying to make yourself feel better. If you hate yourself for your bad behavior, thoughts, or feelings, you're really telling yourself that you're "better than that," and the more intensely you hate yourself, the more powerful your conviction that you're not the man or woman you're presenting yourself to be. But here's the problem: although this process may bring you relief in the short term, eventually it just leaves you just feeling bad.

Whenever you start immediately beating yourself up for your flaws, pause, breathe, and introspect. Understand that your dysfunctional behaviors, thoughts, and feelings are a road map . . . a map that can take you to psychological treasures buried long ago.

> *A dysfunctional behavior, thought or feeling represents a big "X" on your psychological "treasure map" that tells you, "DIG HERE!" And if you do this with intention and persistence, you're bound to hit pay dirt. Ignoring these clues may bring relief in the short run, but it also ensures that your underlying feelings stay dormant. Unless they're exposed, they'll remain firmly in place, waiting to be activated over and over again.*

Dysfunction is really a cry for attention. Babies in distress don't have the words to tell you exactly what's wrong with them. Are they hungry? Do they have gas? Are they wet? Are they sick? Are they cranky? Only careful attention will tell you the answer. It's a baby's cries, however, that tell you to check things out and determine what's up. It's the same with your dysfunctional behaviors. They're cries from the depths of your soul. Even as they loudly protest, "Go away and leave me alone!," deep down they're begging for you to take heed.

We decide upon self-exploration when we finally tell ourselves "No more!" and then develop the courage to challenge the behaviors that we've engaged in for years or even decades. This process is tremendously complicated because it requires that we become aware of three psychological time zones—our present, our past, and our hoped-for future—simultaneously. You must revisit your past from the vantage point of the observing present. Self-exploration entails using a type of psychological "time machine" so you can your connect present behaviors, thoughts, and feelings to their genetic beginnings.

If you turn away from this type of exploration, you'll continue on the same old path of hiding the ugly, shameful parts of yourself and then acting as if those parts don't exist in the first place. Not only will you hide your shame, you'll react to its influence by overcompensating. If you feel worthless, you'll show the world how superior you are through arrogance. If you're ashamed sexually, you'll have indiscriminate sex. If you have homosexual thoughts, you may join an anti-gay hate group.

As our former president Bill Clinton learned only too well, it's not the crime—it's the cover-up that causes the real problems. Yes, you *are* flawed—plain and simple—as all of us are, but your attempts to cover up your "humanness" are often much more of a problem than the original issue that you're hiding from.

This is why your very dysfunction provides an invaluable opportunity. It's because of your dysfunction that the opportunity for salvation presents itself. When uncomfortable unconscious feelings compel you to act in dysfunctional ways, you can either ignore or rationalize them away—or you can start on a journey of self-exploration that will ultimately lead you to self-integration and self-actualization. And it's when you make the latter choice that you'll truly be able to say, "My defenses let me down—*thank goodness!*"

take a moment...

1. Can you list two or three traits/behaviors that could be considered as "X"s on your treasure map?

   a. As you examine these traits or behaviors, see if you can move past the obvious explanations that you often use to explain these things to yourself and to others (such as "Things happen" or "Nobody's perfect" or "I only get drunk when I'm with my friends"). Now search for a deeper feeling and explanation for these problematic traits or behaviors.

   b. Try to access the part of you that prevents you from feeling your emotions. If you can, try to remember how old were you when you incorporated this defense?

How we fight
awareness

Let's continue on in your quest to achieve awareness. You possess a strong drive toward the attainment of good feelings. You feel great when you accomplish a difficult task, write the perfect paragraph, or pick out a gift that brings tears of joy. You kiss loved ones because it warms your heart to do so.

It's the insecure, self-loathing, hateful, jealous, angry, envious, doubting, paranoid, self-deprecating feelings that are the "buzz killers." It's a dark day when these unsavory thoughts and feelings come knocking at your psychological door, and you will bring the full force of your psychological abilities to bear to keep these intruders out of your awareness.

These defenses act like an executive assistant to a powerful CEO who all calls and visitors so the "Big Cheese" doesn't have to be bothered with the riffraff (uncomfortable feelings). And a really good assistant will do this without the boss being aware of it.

Let's look at three unconscious strategies you may be using to hide from your uncomfortable feelings: crawling inside your head, talking away your feelings, and metamorphosis.

Crawling Inside Your Head

Using your intellect to ward off uncomfortable feelings is a common—and effective—defense. We all know people who are completely cut off from their feelings. These people reflect cool steel. Instead of acknowledging and feeling their feelings, they move them "upstairs" and think them away. Because emotions have proved too disappointing and hurtful, these people shut them down automatically.

Katie was very adroit at using this defense. She came to therapy because she was lonely and desperate to be in a relationship. I was somewhat puzzled at her predicament because, at first glance, she made a marvelous impression. She was physically beautiful, intelligent, kind, and compassionate, and she had a wicked sense of humor. Under her physical beauty and vivacious personality, however, lurked a pessimistic, insecure woman.

Whenever Katie felt emotionally threatened, her formidable intellect came to the fore, and she felt very threatened by men she was attracted to. She desired men but also feared them. She would analyze each potentially romantic situation so rigorously that any initial attraction eventually evaporated. She scrutinized and strategized every possible relationship outcome: "If I do A, what are all the possible consequences? What if I do B?" and so on. Her elaborate scenarios invariably led to the same types of conclusions:

- "He won't like me."

- "He'll cheat on me."

- "He'll reject me."

- "He already has a girlfriend."

- "He's just coming out of a relationship."

- "He's gay."

- "He has intimacy issues."

- "He doesn't make enough money."

While the details would differ, the anticipated endgame was always the same—humiliation, rejection, and a broken heart.

The eventual outcome of Katie's obsessive thinking was paralysis. She would shut down emotionally before a relationship had a chance of blossoming into something meaningful. After her elaborate risk analyses, a man who initially looked fun and sexy, and who might very well have been interested in her, would look dangerous and menacing. Her unsuspecting suitor would sense her negative vibe and react accordingly. And at this point, the outcome she had predicted—"No man will be interested in me"—became a reality.

"Thank God," she would think, "that I never allowed myself to really feel something for that guy!"

When things would finally go south, she wasn't devastated because she was prepared. Her intellect had once again kept her safe. Stopping the process before it had a chance to unfold invariably kept her safe. Alone and unhappy, but safe.

Talking Your Feelings Right Out of Your Head

Excessive talking is another strategy for keeping uncomfortable feelings at bay. Excessive taking has the (often-desired) effect of preventing unwanted feelings from breaking into your consciousness. Most of us know people who just can't seem to keep quiet. Words leap out of their mouths. There's even a term for it—"logorrhea," or "diarrhea of the mouth"! They fear silence. It arouses anxiety in them because silence gives their listeners a chance to think. Normally, allowing someone else a chance to think is a good thing, but these people fear that if others are given a chance to think: "They'll see right through me and realize how flawed I really am."

> *When you feel understood, your need to act out*
> *in dysfunctional ways immediately subsides.*
> *Shame, humiliation, and rejection fade away.*
> *You no longer need to keep people away or to try*
> *to divert their attention toward something else.*

Metamorphosis

My client Robert appeared uncharacteristically uncomfortable as he walked into my office. As the session progressed, it became apparent that his discomfort centered on the fact that he was attracted to a woman whom his roommate once dated. He feared that I would disapprove of him for having these feelings. These uncomfortable feelings set in motion a series of neurotic behaviors: he smiled nervously as he spoke, his speech was rambling and pressured, he wouldn't make eye contact, he had trouble sitting still, he kept laughing inappropriately—and he downplayed his feelings and intentions by insisting that his feelings weren't really that strong and that all he wanted to do was to take her out for coffee someday.

Right before my eyes, a confident, intelligent, successful thirty-five-year-old man turned into a fumbling, uncertain, insecure little boy.

> *Neurosis can be defined as an attempt to manipulate thoughts or feelings with your mind so you transform them into something more palatable. Instead of allowing your thoughts and feelings conscious exposure, you use a type of mental gymnastics to change, minimize, distort, or repress them.*

Neurotic thinking and behavior stem from your inability to accept and deal with your feelings exactly as they present themselves, and Robert was doing a marvelous job of demonstrating this. His real feelings were: "I really like this girl, and I think she likes me. I'd love to go out with her. She turns me on mentally, emotionally, and physically. I want this to work out, and I think there's a strong possibility that it can."

But he feared that I would think poorly of him if he followed through with his desires. In response to those thoughts, Robert exhibited a variety of neurotic behaviors, such as:

- **Soft-pedaling his plans to ask her out**, to make me believe that he only wants to be friends and that he's not really asking her on a formal date

- **Inappropriate smiles** so he appears nice and less threatening

- **Fidgeting** to distract my attention to something else and to release nervous energy

- **Avoiding eye contact** to avoid seeing my reactions to his plans, and possibly my disapproval. Also, averting his eyes is a sign of passivity—once again, an attempt to appear less threatening.

Keep in mind that Robert was acting this way with me, his therapist—someone with whom he was supposed to feel accepted and safe. If he could have looked at his dilemmas objectively, he might have concluded that dating this girl wasn't worth the strain it would put on his friendship and he might have decided not to go out with her. On the other hand, he could have made the decision to approach his roommate honestly and talk about his feelings so he wouldn't have to sneak around behind his friend's back. If he had done that, he might have learned that his roommate was fine with them dating, or it might have turned out that his roommate hated the idea. Either way, Robert would have had the information he needed to proceed in a direct, mature way.

> *The neurotic constellation of behaviors involves attempts to wrap your mind around uncomfortable thoughts and feelings and to transform them into something less threatening.*

It's important that you begin to develop the ability to observe yourself when uncomfortable feelings wash over you.

When you feel anxiety well up, pay attention and monitor how it impacts your behavior. The goal is to allow your adult psychology to exist alongside your uncomfortable feelings. It's critical that you incorporate your anxiety into the totality of your conscious, adult self. Without this consolidation, your anxiety will split off and catastrophize possible outcomes, and this invariably leads to dysfunctional thoughts, feelings, and behaviors. Psychological integration is an essential part of your emotional and psychological growth and health.

take a moment...

1. Can you identify a defense
   that you typically use to help
   you move away from uncomfortable feelings?

2. How does this defense mani-
   fest itself? For example, do
   you talk a lot? Do you mum-
   ble? Do you avoid making or
   answering phone calls?

3. Can you access the feelings
   that you're trying to avoid
   when you engage in such defenses? What are the core
   feelings that lie beneath these
   defenses?

10 RAID

Your defenses are like a Geiger counter—the closer you come to exposing them, the stronger and more active they become. Your goal is to identify your defenses and to understand your uncomfortable feelings instead of continuing with your defensive reactions to them, because this leads to dysfunctional behaviors.

Steve exemplified this dynamic. All of his romantic relationships ended within months after they began. It wasn't that he was bereft of opportunities. Women were highly attracted to him. He had looks, intelligence, personality, and a highly respected job as a director of music videos. Still, his relationships started well but invariably ended poorly. His problems with women started from the get-go.

For Steve, as for most of us, the first relationship he had with the opposite sex was with his mother, and many of the same dynamics that took place in that relationship eventually got played out in his current ones. When his parents divorced when he was five, his angry and bitter mother received full custody. Without her husband around to balance her emotions, she released a flood of previously dormant anger onto Steve, and being on the receiving end of her tongue-lashings was an all-too-common experience for him.

Her message was loud and consistent. *Steve* was responsible for her misery. *He* was the reason she was depressed. *He* was the reason she wasn't more successful in her job. But her accusations were maddeningly confusing. On one hand,

Steve felt small and pathetic, defenseless against his aggressive and irrational mother. On the other hand, since she constantly blamed him for all her misery, he felt like an evil Superman who was imbued with incredible powers that were capable of causing grief and despair. To add to his confusion, he actually began to wish that bad things would happen to her—but imagine his horror when (according to her) those wishes would come true!

This sense of malevolent omnipotence (that bad things happened *because* of him, while good things happened *in spite* of him) eventually and inevitably crept into all of Steve's romantic relationships. In the beginning, things always went well. Excitement reigned and expectations were easily met. During this honeymoon stage, he was able to develop genuinely positive feelings. As the relationship moved along its natural course, however, things began to change. Steve would feel pressured to maintain the positive feelings that he genuinely felt. As soon as a woman started to develop feelings for him, a powerful sense of obligation overcame him. All of a sudden, he *had* to act lovingly. He *had* to pick the perfect restaurant, he *had* to pick out a birthday gift that she would truly love, and he *had* to constantly say and do the right thing. It was as if ten-year-old Steve took over the driver's seat of his psyche, and this insecure little boy was terrified. He knew how pathetically incapable he was of pleasing a woman, and he was certain that any attempt he made to do so would ultimately fail.

So Steve always found himself locked into an untenable situation. The harder he tried not to disappoint, the more he felt certain that sooner or later he would. Consequently, he would distance himself emotionally, which (understandably) upset his partner, who would voice her displeasure. But her unhappiness would only confirm his feelings of inadequacy and the vicious circle would start. He would pull back even more, which would lead to more anger and disappointment from his partner. Before long, Steve would start resenting her for what she had come to represent—an insatiable person whom he could never please. It was at this point that he would actually end up hating her for loving him—but love was exactly what he had been hoping for when he had first started dating her! Eventually, the romantic relationship would implode under the weight of this emotional "passion play."

Unconscious feelings are like cockroaches that live in the crevices of our mind. Hidden from the light of consciousness, they're free to roam our psyche and infect our self-concepts and self-esteem by whispering messages like:

- "You're a loser."

- "You're pathetic."

- "You're useless."

- "You're a burden."

- "You're ugly."

- "You'll always be a failure."

- "Your only use is as a sex object."

- "No one loves you or will ever love you."

- "You can never make anyone happy."

Cultivating conscious awareness entails shining a bright light into the "cockroach-infested room" of our consciousness. The problem is that, at the first hint of illumination, the roaches skitter under the baseboards, away from our view. This is why it's so difficult to get a good look at the full scope of your psychology. Every time you try to see what's there, your uncomfortable feelings run for cover.

During one session with Steve, I was able to catch a good look at one of his bigger "roaches." He was complaining about how unhappy he was with his girlfriend of six months and was convinced that things couldn't work out. He was presenting well-thought-out arguments to support his conclusion when he inadvertently blurted out, "I just know that I could never be enough for her." Aha! A cockroach that wasn't able to escape by scurrying away. This is like striking psychological oil, and I wasn't about to let this "cockroach" slip away. I asked Steve to verbalize how he *felt* about never being enough for her. I didn't want an *explanation* (an intellectual answer, which was what his unconscious defensive self wanted). Instead, I wanted to know what *feelings* were lurking underneath.

After some hesitation, Steve replied, "She's way too materialistic for me. She's used to a much better lifestyle than I could ever give her."

I then asked him to tell me how he felt about her perceived materialism.

"That ungrateful bitch," he erupted. "Fuck her! Who is she to tell me that what I have isn't enough for her? I make three times as much money as she does! Who needs her anyway?!"

I felt that we were getting close to some core feelings. So I asked him to describe his feelings about his pronouncements, not in terms of what *she* was like but rather how *he* felt in relation to her by using "I" language and speaking in the first person.

After a great deal of coaxing and with much discomfort, he finally muttered, "I know that I can never please Julie."

This statement represented a step deeper. I had him repeat this statement over and over again. Finally, he said with conviction, "I can never please Julie!"

"Why?" I asked. "And tell me in the first person. Close your eyes and turn inward."

When Steve spoke again, it was clear that core feelings were finally being uncovered and that hidden feelings that he had been fiercely avoiding were beginning to surface.

"I'm worthless," he whispered in a barely audible voice. "I'm a failure. I'm less than a man. I'm a fraud, and sooner or later Julie will figure this out. I know that I could never truly make her happy." Tears began streaming down his face. Standing before him were the demons that he had spent a lifetime trying to keep at bay.

I had Steve repeat his statements verbatim over and over. As he complied, repeating, "I'm a loser! I'm a fraud! I'm worthless!," it was like squeezing the pus out of a festering psychological wound. Ten . . . twenty . . . thirty times he repeated the awful feelings that he had spent a lifetime running from.

> **Repeatedly voicing uncomfortable thoughts and feelings aloud forces them out of your psychological "crevices." By verbalizing these thoughts and feelings in the first person, you're essentially calling out your unconscious fears and forcing them to stand front and center. This shows that you're no longer afraid of them and are willing to integrate them into the totality of who you are.**

—\\\\\\—

> **A primary goal of achieving psychological health is to move toward a fully conscious state— Awareness (with a capital A). Fully aware individuals integrate the unconscious with the conscious and can identify and feel their feelings in their pure form and in real time.**

Integrating all of these feelings meant allowing Steve's repressed ten-year-old child to coexist with the thirty-seven-year-old adult sitting before me. I was convinced that ten-year-old Steve—scared, angry, insecure, and intent on preventing any more hurt and pain—would be no match for the intelligent, creative, popular, dynamic, kind, considerate thirty-seven-year-old Steve. Why did that ten-year-old boy still have so much influence? *Because he had never been challenged.* For almost three decades, he's been ruling Steve's unconscious domain, but now the adult Steve—conscious and strong Steve—had entered Steve's psychological scene, and ten-year-old Steve was being confronted by a strong, powerful man ... adult Steve.

The result of this union was integration. Previously these two "Steves" had led separate existences. Integration did not mean that ten-year-old Steve would be destroyed. That would be impossible, unnecessary, and wrong. Ten-year-old Steve deserved to exist and deserved to be valued and loved—which his mother had never done properly. That little boy still existed, but now he wasn't all by himself. Now he had the adult Steve by his side.

Becoming aware is a terrifically difficult and painful task. The psychological maze we construct to avoid these feelings is truly brilliant. Once in it, getting out makes solving a Rubik's Cube puzzle seem easy. The difficulty in this process stems from the fact that the only way out is to consciously accept the very thoughts and feelings that motivated us to build the maze in the first place!

In Steve's case, he had to fully accept his deepest fears—that he *was* worthless, that he *was* a failure, that he *was* less than a man, and that he could never please a woman. As bizarre as it may sound, it was only through *accepting* these awful feelings that he was able to experience new feelings of being valuable, successful, worthwhile, and masculine.

In a roundabout way, accepting his shameful self was actually a form of self-love. In his acceptance, the adult Steve figuratively put his arm around the scared, shame-filled ten-year-old Steve and told him, "I know who you are and I accept you. I'm not going to push you away as if you make me sick. Instead,

I'm going to embrace and love you in all of your (perceived) worthlessness, and, in this process, I'll also show you what a big strong man you can be—and in fact *are*."

We all carry thoughts that are difficult to tolerate, and we usually try to either talk ourselves out of them or to overcompensate for them. Let's look at one example of how to work through this. Here's the difficult thought:

- "I'm afraid to tell Peggy that I'm upset about her canceling plans with me at the last minute."

Instead of rationalizing these feelings away, stop and see if you can identify the fear and anxiety:

- "If I tell Peggy I'm upset with her, she'll reject me."

Again, instead of rationalizing this feeling, you want to move toward it. An excellent way to do this is by vocalizing the deeper feelings that are lurking underneath your feelings. Put them into words and say them out loud:

- "She'll reject me, because if I'm not always nice to her, she'll have no use for me."

You need to guard against talking yourself out of this deeper feeling by telling yourself that you're being silly for having it in the first place. Now move toward identifying your real core feelings and moving toward them, again vocalizing them:

- "She'll have no use for me because I'm not that funny or smart or outgoing. I have so little value as a person that I have to put my feelings aside so I won't be rejected."

And this is where you need to stay for a while. At this point, you need to repeat the core truth you've uncovered aloud between fifty and one hundred times.

> **When you catch a glimpse of a psychological "roach,"
> you need to examine it in the light of your Awareness so
> you can flush out its true meaning. Moving toward
> your pain exposes it to your consciousness.
> When you avoid painful feelings and psychological
> wounds, you treat them as if they're "ugly" and
> "shameful" and deserve to be locked away in
> the closet of your mind. But you can heal your
> psychological wounds when you make a commitment to
> never again treat them with disgust or shame.**

I'm aware of how complicated this may sound. I view defensive behaviors and feelings not as things that are bad but rather as things that are kind and decent because they're committed to protecting us from harm—whether real or imagined. This is why self-exploration is such a courageous adventure. It can take you to dark places, but it's a worthy and noble task.

So, commit to facing your deepest fears. Commit to understanding and loving your "roaches" instead of instantly squashing them. When you're able to do this, you're showing yourself compassion and care—truly a high form of self-love.

take a moment...

1. Think of something that you
   want to do but that's making
   you afraid to move forward.
   Can you list five specific steps
   you could take in the service
   of achieving your goal?

2. With each individual step,
   what do you foresee as the
   consequences of failure?

3. On a scale of 1 to 10, with
   1 being least probable and 10
   being most probable, write
   down how likely it is that
   your worst-case scenario
   might happen.

It's no big deal
I'm only depressed

Boxers say that they know that their skills have diminished when they can see a punch (an opening that will let them connect with the opponent's chin) but can no longer make it. I often see this problem with my clients. They sit across from me in total frustration because they know that something's wrong with the way they're navigating their lives, but they can't seem to implement what they want to do, what they know they should do, or what they dream of doing. Even though these patients want and can clearly articulate their goals, they can't move from the level of wants and desires to action. However clearly they're able to hear the music in their heads, they're unable to play the notes.

When you're burdened with depression, even routine aspects of life become difficult. Depression can get such a strong grip on us that it can actually impact our will to live. It can take young, energetic individuals full of life and ambition, and transform them into empty shells—listless, helpless, and hopeless.

Depression had Maria firmly in its grasp. At first glance, you would think she was living a charmed life. At thirty-four, she was in her prime—exceptionally beautiful, married to a successful businessman, and mother to three loving children. Behind the façade, however, lived a sad and severely insecure woman. She was convinced that she was nothing but a burden to those around her. A typical day consisted of her waking up, taking her children to school, and then going back home to spend the rest of the day in bed. Thoughts of dying often left her with a feeling of peace.

As Maria's therapy progressed, a great deal of repressed anger began to surface. Anger—or, more precisely, unexpressed and unprocessed anger—is an essential ingredient of depression.

Through the years, she had spent enormous amounts of psychological resources trying to repress these feelings. Anger was never allowed in her childhood, and she had numerous memories to remind her of just how destructive and ugly it could be.

It can be especially difficult to access feelings of anger when they're directed toward loved ones (Mom, Dad, spouse, partner), and if these feelings do surface, they're quickly and forcefully repressed. However, unexpressed feelings fester in our psychology like undigested meals. They can infect our psychology so profoundly that we end hating ourselves for harboring (what we judge as) such "awful" feelings in the first place. As we should expect, based on what we know about the lifelong impact of childhood experiences, parents are often the most challenging target of unresolved and unconscious anger, but it can be emotionally overwhelming to be saddled with such feelings.

> *One hallmark of emotional and psychological health is the ability to "hate your parents well."*
> *"Hating a parent well" means hating them without hating* yourself *for hating them.*

What's problematic, however, is not anger itself, but the repression of anger. In reality, anger is neutral. It can be destructive or constructive, depending on your ability to first acknowledge the feelings, then to tolerate them and, ultimately, to express them in a healthy way.

> *Depression can be understood as a verb—*
> *literally, "to depress one's feelings."*
> *When uncomfortable feelings enter consciousness,*
> *the depressed person (unconsciously) pushes them*
> *away from awareness as quickly as possible.*

Repressing feelings takes a tremendous amount of energy. It's like trying to stuff a huge down pillow into a soft-drink bottle. But the work doesn't stop there, because once you've managed to repress the feelings, you must remain vigilant to make sure that they stay repressed. If you let up for even a moment, you risk having them escape back up into your awareness. This is why depressed people claim they're exhausted. No wonder! They're using every last bit of their energy struggling to feel happy!

Suppose I have hate-filled feelings toward my father but can't tolerate acknowledging these feelings consciously. In my effort to live a reasonably happy life—one that's in harmony with my need to see myself as a man who honors his father— my unconscious mind does its best to keep these feelings buried. Or, if they sneak up into my consciousness, I quickly rationalize them away ("He tried the best he could, so stop hating him!").

But even if I do succeed in repressing my anger, it'll still exert its influence on my feelings and behaviors. For example, I may find that I get angry with my father for "no apparent reason." I may become irritated at the sound of his voice, or I'll catch myself criticizing the way he dresses or the car he drives. Perhaps I won't call him as often as I used to. I may even move to another city just so I don't have to see him.

These reactions may appear unreasonable, but that's because I'm unable to acknowledge the negative feelings on which my actions are based. Eventually I'll end up criticizing myself for what appears to be unjust and mean behavior on my part. "What kind of son am I?" I'll wonder. "How can I be so mean and judgmental?" The only conclusion I'll be able to come up with is that, since he hasn't done anything to deserve such harsh treatment (at least in present time), it stands to reason that *I* must be the awful one. At this point, the circle completes itself: my feelings of hatred toward my father become feelings of hatred towards myself.

> *One major yet unwelcome side effect of repressing negative feelings is that your good feelings will get repressed along with your uncomfortable ones. Your psyche can't pick and choose which feelings get repressed. Emotions are like a ship—you may try to sink just the stern, but you'll find that the rest of the boat goes under as well. This is why depression makes us unable to experience feelings of pleasure and happiness. It's not that we don't want to feel good feelings, or that there isn't anything in our life that's joyful. It's that depression acts like a thick blanket that mutes our entire emotional spectrum. In the process of repressing negative feelings, we unwittingly sacrifice our positive ones as well. The unconscious mind subjects us to a terrible deal because the tactics it uses to make us feel better also prevent us from feeling the joy that we were hoping to access in the first place!*

Maria felt alone in the world, and she desperately needed a space where she could feel safe enough to feel the full spectrum of her emotions. Therapy provided such a place. My listening—careful, caring listening—provided her a setting where she was able to access her long-dormant feelings. When they bubbled up, I listened with focused attention. I let her know that they didn't repel me. I showed empathy and compassion toward the feelings that she was ashamed of and that she felt deserved to be locked away.

My acceptance of her , and of all of her feelings, brought her a profound sense of relief. Her need to actively repress her feelings lessened, and she discovered that the less she repressed her negative emotions, the more other feelings like joy and happiness—those "bystander emotions" that had been getting caught in the undertow along with her negative ones—began to surface.

No matter how much Maria felt understood by me, her therapy would have been useless if she could experience new behaviors and emotions only within the therapeutic setting. The point of therapy is for patients to be able to transfer the feelings and behavioral changes that take place in sessions into their everyday lives, and this is exactly what Maria was able to. She no longer saw anger as the vile, destructive, out-of-control emotion that she had grown up with. She finally realized that it was possible to feel and express those feelings without destroying others or being destroyed by them.

This newfound freedom enabled Maria to develop "psychological backbone." The more she evolved, the more she stopped being a doormat to her husband, her mother, her siblings, her friends, and her children. This transformation caused a sea change in her relationships. For example, when her husband criticized her, she would stand up for herself instead of cowering in fear and humiliation. When her children were disrespectful, she punished them instead of locking herself in her room to cry. And when she told her mother how she felt about her childhood and her mother tried to change the subject or to minimize what Maria was saying, she insisted on being heard.

When you're able to access and tolerate angry feelings, you'll be able to be a kinder, happier, and more loving person—because the very thing that you've been fearing turns out to be the cure. The more you express *all* of your feelings, even the ones that you feel are "ugly" or "nasty," the more your depression will lift, and the more joy and jubilation—major casualties of depression—will spring back to life. You'll begin to embrace life and will look to the future with hope instead of dread. Your deepest, darkest fears will turn into beacons that will guide you out of depression and into a fully actualized life.

take a moment...

1. Think back to your childhood. Can you list any feelings (for example, joy, anger, envy, sadness, pride, hate, or fear) that you weren't allowed to express?

2. Can you identify any members of your family who were or are depressed? If so, what emotions do you think they were or still are repressing?

3. Suppose you could go to the people in your life for whom you've had those feelings that you weren't allowed to express, and could express those feelings to them directly—but imagine that one minute after you speak, they'll completely forget what you had told them. Now write down what you would say to them.

take a moment...

4. If you suffer from depression, try to conceptualize
   your depression as an active
   process. Assume for a moment that the reason you feel
   down is that you're *depressing* your uncomfortable feelings. See if you can access the
   uncomfortable feelings, and
   if you can, speak them aloud
   to yourself. (Some common examples might include:
   "I'm worthless," "I hate my
   parent(s)," or "I'm a fraud, and
   I'm going to be found out for
   all the world to see.")

_____

_____

_____

_____

_____

_____

_____

_____

_____

_____

_____

_____

_____

_____

_____

12 When you
have an answer for everything

Let's look at some other common psychological defenses that you may use to keep uncomfortable thoughts and feelings at bay.

Obsessive Compulsive Disorder (OCD)

People with OCD are cursed with obsessions (uncontrollable thoughts) and compulsions (uncontrolled behaviors). They may wash their hands to the point of making them bleed, or they may make sure that everything is exactly in its place. Even though they realize intellectually just how ludicrous their behavior is, their incessant thoughts (hence "obsessive") *compel* (hence "compulsive") them to perform these rituals.

The benefit of this defense is that the mind becomes so preoccupied with irrational thoughts and behaviors that very little psychological space is left for other uncomfortable (and perhaps forbidden) thoughts such as "I hate my mother," "I have homosexual urges," "The world is dangerous," and so forth. One wonders what thoughts and feelings would percolate up into consciousness if these people's obsessions and compulsions were cured.

Panic Attacks and Anxiety

These people are overpowered by extreme tension and anxiety. They imagine that catastrophic consequences will result from relatively neutral events such as asking someone out on a date, giving a presentation, or meeting a lover's family. People

who suffer from panic attacks and anxiety are constantly imag-
ining stories about how events will unfold—and those stories
always have catastrophic endings.

Panic and anxiety totally crowd out nuance or measured
thinking. Physically, these conditions throw the body into over-
drive, with the anxiety-fueled rush of adrenaline and a racing
heartbeat leaving people feeling as if they're in real danger.

When anxiety and panic set in, any sense of proportion is
lost, as is the ability to be self-reflective, because people are
trying to contain a hurricane in their minds and bodies.

Agoraphobia

Agoraphobics isolate themselves rather than face a world that
they believe to be harsh and judgmental. They're convinced that
if they were to expose themselves to the world, they would
be revealed as the horrible and disgusting people that their
history has led them to believe they are. These people live in a
psychological prison of their own making, and they can't bear
to challenge their (mis)perceptions.

Paranoia

The thoughts and feelings of paranoid individuals are so destructive and overwhelming that they literally "disown" them
and "give" them away to others. Once this is accomplished,
paranoid individuals become convinced that the people upon
whom they've projected their own feelings feel toward them
the way they feel about themselves. Because people who are
paranoid are convinced that others think poorly of them and
mean to do them harm, they're certainly going to be suspicious
of the thoughts and feelings of others.

However, paranoid people never think of themselves as
paranoid because "You're not paranoid if someone's really following you," and from their perspective, that's exactly what's
happening. They're convinced that other people hate them and

are out to get them when in reality those "other people" are unwittingly mirrors of the paranoid's own self-loathing.

Most people who are insecure carry at least a small degree of paranoia within themselves because insecurities often warp reality toward the negative. When you're hampered by a shredded self-image, it's difficult *not* to believe that everyone you meet isn't in on the secret of all of your bad qualities. You feel worthless and invisible, but at the same time you're convinced that, when you walk into a room, everyone will stop what they're doing, look right at you, and immediately pick up on all of your many flaws. Alcoholics Anonymous has a saying that encapsulates this idea: "I'm a piece of shit at the center of the universe."

Narcissism

Narcissists are so self-absorbed that they're incapable of truly considering and empathizing with the feelings of others. They fit the bill of someone who's "a legend in their own mind." They're fighting desperately to keep the haunting voice of their unconscious away from their awareness. But hidden within these arrogant and seemingly uncaring individuals are people with feet of clay. They feel a sense of entitlement yet are full of (unconscious) rage because their feelings of primacy in the world have been violated (for example, when a child is displaced as the "prince" or "princes in the family on the birth of a new baby).

As adults, instead of relaxing into their life and position, narcissists feel superior and demand adoration irrespective of merit or audience. They avoid real intimacy and instead choose a superior "perch" from which they relate to others. Looking down on the world from their mountaintop prevents others from getting close enough to see the shabby structure that lies hidden behind narcissists' shiny, grandiose exteriors.

Psychosis

Psychosis, which constitutes a "break" from reality, is the most severe defense against feeling uncomfortable thoughts and feelings. Psychotics are so unable to tolerate uncomfortable feelings that they literally "decompensate" into a kind of psychological firestorm and dive into a world of hallucinations, bizarre delusions, and psychological isolation.

The Value of Defenses in Early Life

Most of these defenses were perfectly appropriate and necessary at the time they were formed in childhood. As defenseless children, we don't have the resources to combat dysfunctional adults or environments. We were stuck with whatever environment was presented, whether it was inconsistent, hate-filled, rejecting, emotionally isolating, sexually provocative, or violent. The defenses that we all developed were actually quite brilliant given our limited development and resources. But when childhood defenses follow us into adulthood, problems develop. Early defenses can become so entrenched and so much a part of our psychological fiber that they'll remain intact throughout our lives if we don't let go of them.

You're literally a history book—someone who is carrying within yourself the experiences of thirty, forty, or fifty years of living. The person you are this very moment is an amalgamation of all the experiences you've had throughout your life. These experiences are the building blocks of your personality and psychological makeup. Traumatic incidents or difficult relationships aren't the only causes of the current pain or dysfunction that you may be experiencing—just as a lightning strike isn't the sole cause of a house burning down. It's the fire that follows that completes the devastation.

The neighborhood boy who molested Josh when he was nine robbed him of his innocence and of his trust in others. To be sure, the molestation was horrible in and of itself. And it understandably had a ripple effect in terms of causing unanticipated negative consequences for Josh. Before the molestation, he was happy, carefree, confident, and friendly. Afterward, he became depressed, mistrustful, sexually provocative, and angry. His family and friends didn't know what he had been through. All they saw was someone who had "all of a sudden" become angry and paranoid. Eventually they came to view his mistrust as a character flaw, and they distanced themselves. But this rejection only served to confirm to Josh that the world *was* dangerous and that he should continue to be angry and mistrustful. No doubt the molestation was the inciting event, but how it affected him and how he behaved afterward set in place a vicious and self-reinforcing circle.

These vicious circles are very hard to break. You feel stuck, stuck, stuck:

- "I wish I knew what to do . . . it just seems so hopeless!"

- "My mind goes blank."

- "I have no idea what to do differently."

- "Everyone else has an answer but me."

It's very easy to become discouraged and convinced that your situation is hopeless. But take care that you don't go on telling yourself why things must remain the same, because if you do it long enough, you can become bitter and depressed:

You lament: "I don't make enough money."

Obvious solution: "If you don't like your career choice, go back to school."

Your snap pushback: "I could never do that because _____."

You lament: "He doesn't understand me."

Obvious solution: "Tell him how you really feel."

Your snap pushback: "You've got to be kidding. If I did that, then _____."

—⁂—

You lament: "I hate going to John's mother's house every Sunday!"

Obvious solution: "If you don't really want to go, don't."

Your snap pushback: "You don't understand. If I don't go, then _____."

—⁂—

You lament: "Susan goes out with her friends at least three times a week."

Obvious solution: "If you're not happy with Susan, maybe you should leave her."

Your snap pushback: "I could never do that! She depends on me. Besides, _____."

—⁂—

You lament: "I'm afraid of starting a new business."

Obvious solution: "You hate your present job. You've got a great idea for a product! You should go into business for yourself."

Your snap pushback: "That's crazy! If I tried and the business went under, _____."

—◊—

You lament: "I'm not satisfied with our sex life."

Obvious solution: "If Frank's not a good lover, maybe you should talk to him about it."

Your snap pushback: "How could I tell Frank I'm not happy with his lovemaking? If I did, _____."

Automatic, fear-based responses stop all forward progress. It can be helpful to pay attention to how you respond when others give you suggestions or advice. When your responses are very quick and expressed with intensity and conviction, that's often a sign that defenses are in play. Instead, when someone gives you a suggestion, pause, take a moment, and think through what you're being told. Really listening and thinking doesn't mean that you'll agree with what's being said—it only means that you'll be better able to hear it with nondefensive ears.

> *Reflection before action*
> *is an integral part of emotional health.*

Emotions travel faster than rational thoughts, and it's crucial that you don't let your emotions dominate your life. If I'm a fearful flyer, I may feel certain that when the plane encounters turbulence, it's sure to crash. Initially, my fear races ahead of my rational mind and overtakes my psychology. Thankfully, however, my rational mind eventually catches up and I don't run up and down the aisle screaming that we're facing impending doom. My rational mind steps in and reminds me that the shaking of the plane is due to choppy air and that the plane is built to withstand a hundred times greater stress than what it's currently experiencing.

A pause for rational reflection will give you the opportunity to question whether your fear-driven automatic responses are based on the present circumstances and whether they're proportional to the situation at hand, or not. You may feel mortified when you walk into a room and hear laughter because you "feel" that people are making fun of you. However, taking a moment of calm reflection will allow you to take a sober look at the situation and to consider all the possible reasons for the laughter.

Self-reflection is a key component of change, as when "I know I shouldn't drink, but pass me a beer" turns into "I feel like a beer but I'm not going to have one. I've been drinking way too much and I know it isn't good for me."

Challenging "emotional logic" allows you to bring your adult self forward . . . the self that's telling you to be better. By not solely acting emotionally—in other words, by acting based on feelings rather than on rational thinking—you give yourself a chance to behave differently.

And this is how you learn to play the notes that you hear in your head.

take a moment...

1. If you suffer from one of the conditions described in this chapter, can you connect it to any traumatic events or difficult circumstances in your past? If you can, write down how these changed you. List five of the personal emotional qualities you had before the events and then what changed afterward. For example: "Before the event, I was outgoing; after the event, I became shy and reclusive."

2. Can you identify how those reactive behaviors have helped you to cope?

13 Psychological
nuclear fusion

While it's natural to want to be in meaningful relationships, the closeness that intimacy brings can be intense and discomforting. It's harder to fool people you see or live with every day. You may convince friends that you're a sex machine, but you can't fool a partner who complains that you never want to make love. You may brag that you're impervious to how others see you, but your spouse has to pick up the pieces when you fall apart after an evening with your hypercritical mother. Intimacy has a way of wedging itself into the cracks in your defenses, and this kind of psychological nakedness can be overwhelming.

Fear of exposure can compel you to present a homogenized and pasteurized version of yourself. The "I" that defines you begins to fade away. This can be psychologically terrifying. Imagine that you're drowning in a tumultuous ocean. You're gasping for air and can barely keep your head above water. You're so cold, and you've been in the water for such a long time, that you can't feel any separation between yourself and the water that's surrounding you. In such dire circumstances, you'll understandably grab onto anyone who'll keep you afloat, and all too often it's flawed people—people who alcoholic, abusive, untrustworthy, unfaithful, and so forth—who are your most easily accessible "flotation devices." After all, connections with even severely flawed people are a better alternative than drowning in a sea of loneliness.

Natalie's psychological buoyancy was very shaky. Because

of a toxic and chaotic childhood environment, she was unable to internalize the concept that a solid and whole "Natalie" even existed. Her parents divorced when she was seven, and her father moved away to start another family. Her mother was emotionally fragile and became hyper-emotional at the slightest provocation. Small upsets frequently turned into major uproars. There was no middle ground: minor inconveniences became calamities, and any act of selfishness became a statement of complete uncaring. What's worse, Natalie's mother died in an automobile accident when Natalie was fifteen. Once again, no middle ground.

Natalie felt that she had to be hyper-aware of what others were doing, thinking, and feeling at all times so she could make sure that others around her were happy. Over time, she developed a chameleon-like personality whereby she would mold herself to whomever she was with. She became expert at understanding, anticipating, and complying with the desires of others. If they liked hiking, she liked hiking. If they were politically conservative, she was politically conservative. She was hesitant to put forward her beliefs, be they political, religious or related to current events, especially if they differed from those of the person she was with because she expected rejection and abandonment if she expressed any genuine differences or lack of agreement with others. Of course, had she still been a young, helpless child and at the mercy of the adults around her, her behavior would have been more rational because it would have been a survival mechanism—but she was a full-grown adult. Or rather, a psychological child trapped in the body of an adult.

When I imagined how Natalie would look if her physical appearance reflected her psychological makeup, I saw her as transparent, as if one could see right through her. Another image I had was of a woman with a huge hole in the middle of her chest. All of her painful experiences had left a void where

"Natalie" had once resided, and it was this emptiness that compelled her to fuse with others. On her own, she felt lost and untethered. Only by psychologically merging with another person was she able to feel whole and safe. Unfortunately, this strategy had a limited shelf-life because she would merge so completely that she would inevitably lose herself in the other. This left her feeling as if she were once again drowning, but this time she was submerged in the life of her partner.

The last image I had of her was one of a seductress/viper. Natalie was an expert at drawing people in, but when the closeness became overwhelming she would create distance by flying into venomous rages. She desperately wanted deep connections, but they ultimately left her feeling just as lost.

Monitoring Your Psychological Makeup

Monitor your psychological makeup in your intimate relationships. Do you ever feel an overwhelming need for the other—a need that doesn't seem healthy? Is your self-image defined by how this person sees you? Do you mold your likes and dislikes, or even the makeup of your personality, in order to please and be accepted by this person? Do any of the following relationship strategies sound familiar?

- You lie, either by omission or commission. You stifle your true feelings when they may upset others.

- You make "obligatory calls" to your parents or friends when you know that the person you're calling won't be home because you feel incapable of putting your true self forward. Fearful of rejection, you hide behind voicemail.

- You're unable to defend yourself against criticism. It's difficult for you to stand up for yourself even if in your heart you think that your critic is being irrational, selfish, or cruel. You retreat into silence, become depressed, and/or try to change yourself to meet the needs of others.

• If friends misinterpret an innocent gesture or comment you make to mean something negative, you beat yourself up because you believe that you were wrong and flawed for upsetting them.

• If someone you care about is in a bad mood, you automatically assume that it's because of something you said or did.

• Every day you feel that you have to prove anew that you're good, kind, and decent. You're convinced that other people will always and ultimately judge you based on the last impression you make. If a friend asks for a favor and you're unable to oblige, you fear that you'll be seen as selfish and uncaring, even if in the past you've repeatedly shown yourself to be reliable and caring. In your mind, the totality of who you are is always measured by your most recent act.

• You feel threatened when your partner or close friends have independent interests. You feel anxious if your husband wants to work on his car, play golf or basketball, see a friend, etc., or if your wife wants to take a class or join a book club. Their independence threatens the fusion you desire. You secretly believe that their emotional, intellectual, and spiritual growth will lead them to realize how inadequate you really are.

• When you plan to see a movie or have dinner with

friends, you always go along with their choices. You rarely speak up and express your wants and desires.

- You put up with being treated outrageously by, for example, staying with a girlfriend who's dating other guys, or being "understanding" when a boyfriend often goes out drinking without you.

- You choose careers, spouses, religions, and political affiliations to please your parents, even if those choices aren't ones that you really want or believe in.

All of these behaviors contribute to fragmenting your identity, so much so that eventually you can become unsure of your purpose in life. This is why cults and fundamentalist religions can be so alluring: individuals with a weak sense of self can find themselves attracted to persons or groups that promise acceptance and direction. People who have fragmented identities and who are drowning in purposelessness believe for the sake of believing because this gives them a sense of meaning where none previously existed. They fall in love with leaders' personalities (and with whatever ideas the leaders may espouse) because those figures embody all the qualities that they desire.

The more I study the inner workings of the human psyche, the more I realize how much it mimics the physical universe. Take, for example, our solar system. We have a star (the sun) and planets that revolve around it. The difference between a star and a planet is that a star can generate and give off great amounts of energy and heat. A simple explanation is that for a star to become a star, a high degree of mass needs to exist. Once mass reaches a critical point, it will start a process whereby the gravity from the center begins to pull matter inward from the periphery. This process, which is called nuclear fusion, is the key component in "star making," and through it, energy and heat are created. Nuclear fusion is such a powerful process that a star can warm planets millions of miles away, and its light can be seen for billions upon billions of miles.

The same process is in play in the human experience. Most of us have both "sun-like" and "planet-like qualities." The question is, which way do you lean?

Are You a "Sun"?

For people to be considered "sun-like," they must possess a substantial amount of psychological "mass." This is generated by a high degree of self-awareness and by living with integrity and vigor. Sun-like people have many interests, hobbies, and intellectual pursuits. They live with passion and creativity and are self-contained, self-rejuvenating, and self-directed. "Suns" generate gravity in that they attract people by their mere presence and being. People are attracted to their power. Suns have direction and are self-assured, confident, and inquisitive. Suns question authority, think "outside the box" and aren't hindered by norms or by what others think they should do. They generate their own light and warmth and don't look to others to provide either.

We all know Suns when we meet them because they shine. They exude a power that's attractive and often awe-inspiring. Their creativity, insight, and passion motivate and inspire others. If they choose to be leaders, they are—and if they don't, others still follow them regardless, either overtly or covertly.

I don't mean to imply that these people are islands unto themselves or that they don't need or want others. On the contrary, they tend to thrive in the arena of relationships. They tend to be positive, passionate, and synergistic. They seek out other like-minded individuals because they know that together they're greater than the sum of their respective parts. They're happy about the successes of others, and they help them to achieve it in any way possible. They love for the sake of love, and not as a way to resolve unmet psychological needs. They work, live, and love with an internal fire that burns as brightly as the stars they are.

Are You a "Planet"?

Planets are unable to generate true warmth or light. "Planet" people have little psychological mass in the sense that there is little that truly animates or inspires them. For this reason, they need and seek proximity to a Sun. Because Planets need warmth to survive, when they encounter a Sun, they become keenly attuned to what the Sun is doing, thinking, and feeling. Planets fear that if they stray too far, they'll lose contact with the Sun's gravitational field and will be left alone in a dark and cold world.

We know Planets when you meet them. Like Natalie, Planets are overly compliant and agreeable. They're always trying to "do the right thing." They spend so much time thinking about others that they never get a chance to determine what it is that *they* feel passionate about. Planets engage in relationships in a parasitic manner. They resent or are terrified by the successes of others because these are reminders of what they can't have. Success only highlights the gulf that Planets perceive between themselves and others, but it's a gulf that they don't know how to bridge. Whenever Planets realize that they're more interested in the Suns around them than the Suns are interested in them, they're overcome with disappointment, terror, and depression.

Even Planets Can Become Suns

Like most of us, you're probably somewhere in the middle. However, the more you evolve spiritually, intellectually, and emotionally, the more Sun-like you will become. Once you figure out that when you embrace who you are, trust your instincts, chase your failures, and, after each success, quickly move on to what's next:

- ◆ You'll wake up every morning full of hope and anticipation.

- ◆ You'll look forward to what's around the next bend, not with fear but with quiet confidence.

- ◆ You'll move past the circumstances of your past and embrace the future.

What's more, ancient psychological injuries, big and small, will become smaller and smaller parts of your psychological landscape. It isn't that their importance is diminished; it's that the more you evolve and grow intellectually, emotionally, and spiritually, the bigger your world will become and the less influence the past will have on you.

As your personal evolution continues, your growth will reach a point of "critical psychological mass." Without even being aware of it, you'll begin to engage in "psychological nuclear fusion." In other words, you'll start to become a Sun. (As an aside, this is how you felt when you first came into the world, back when you ruled it by way of your childhood omnipotence. The only difference is that now you're actually creating and defining your world instead of merely *fantasizing* that you are.)

When Natalie and I started working together, she was like Neptune—a distant planet, small, cold, and isolated. As time went on, however, she began to gain psychological mass. The experience of feeling heard and unconditionally cared for provided her with the psychological elements that she needed to grow stronger. She began to ask for what *she* wanted. She spoke up when others hurt her. She expressed opinions without worrying about how they would be received. At work, she started to take on more difficult assignments that required her to lead, motivate, and discipline.

Like all of us, Natalie had always contained within herself the qualities that would enable her to become a Sun. She just needed to access them. By focusing less on what others were thinking, doing, and feeling, she found within herself the ability to mine her own psychological "gold." Instead of continuing to throw in her lot with people who would allow her to orbit around them, she began to realize that she could generate her own heat, and she thereby became more selective about the people she connected with.

Will Natalie ever become a Sun? That remains to be seen. Like most of us, she's so close and yet so far. She has moved up a few notches, no doubt. As of this writing, I would classify her as a "Jupiter," only a step or two away from reaching critical mass. Becoming a Sun is no easy accomplishment (which is why there's an eight-to-one ratio of planets to sun in our solar system). But the more you invest in yourself . . . the more you cherish and love who you are . . . and the more you challenge yourself to get past your defenses and into your joy, passion, and destiny . . . the closer you'll get to creating your very own psychological nuclear fusion.

take a moment...

1. Do you have any "Suns" in your life? Write down what qualities these people have that make you want to revolve around them.

2. List five psychological qualities that these Suns possess that you feel you lack.

3. List five steps that you can take that will start you on the path toward psychological nuclear fusion.

4. Was there ever a time in your life when you felt complete and completely self-contained? Write about that time—about what was going on then and about what's different now.

14 I just
forgot it!

By now you're getting a clearer picture of the structure of your psychology and of how it impacts your perception of yourself and your world. The culmination of the entirety of your experiences has led you to this moment, and you're beginning to understand exactly how these experiences have affected you. Without conscious attention, the many and varied psychological defenses that you've erected can keep your dreams forever out of reach. They'll propel you toward mediocrity by sabotaging you at every turn, and, if you aren't careful, you'll wake up and find that there's a huge gap between the way that you've envisioned how your life was supposed to turn out and the way that you're actually living it.

Susan embodied this concept. Her defenses were strong and formidable. A crack team of Navy Seals couldn't have penetrated the protective wall she had built around herself. She was a "Yes, but . . ." person who had an arsenal of excuses as to why she was incapable of changing the problems that she so fiercely complained about.

She often expounded on how desperately she needed to change her life. Sessions would often begin with her plopping down on my couch with a look of utter dejection and saying, "Nothing new to report except that I actually feel worse than I did last time." Everything that I tried to offer that might have helped—compassion, empathy, interpretations, cognitive reasoning—proved ineffective. Eventually I resorted to strict problem-solving. If she complained that she couldn't get a date, we would discuss where she could meet men, how she could show that she was interested, and so on. If she was having problems with her family, we would discuss strategies whereby she could be effective in dealing with them. We weren't doing particularly deep psychological work per se, but that was where I thought I could be most effective.

Career issues were a frequent topic of discussion. She worked in a family-owned company where her job responsibilities were repetitive and boring. She complained that she had to "find something else to do, or I'm going to go crazy!" She found living surrounded by her family and isolated from the world suffocating. Over and over she lamented, "I hate my job. I can't stand it any longer! You don't understand how depressing it is to go into work every day. I've got to do something!"

When I asked her what she would do instead, she surprised me by having an answer at the ready. She wanted to work in the film industry. In particular, she wanted to produce feature-length films. Right after she had left college and before she had begun working for her family, she had worked at a studio and loved it. She very much regretted having decided to leave the entertainment industry to work in her family business, and she kept dreaming of giving it another try.

We explored specific strategies that could turn her dream into reality, but it seemed as if the more we did this, the more her fears and insecurities pushed back. Eventually I was able to help her break through her defenses, and she agreed to reach out to friends who worked in the entertainment industry to see if they knew of any opportunities. This was a huge win because she had moved from thinking about something to doing something.

As luck would have it, a well-connected friend of hers was able to arrange an interview with a studio executive who just happened to be looking for someone with Susan's exact qualifications.

At this point, her fears erupted more strongly than ever.

Overpowered by apprehension, she realized that walking up to the edge of this cliff was giving her psychological vertigo. Enveloped in fear and doubt, she began obsessing about all the reasons why things wouldn't work out: she hadn't been on an interview in years, she wasn't confident about her resume, and she was convinced that she would make a bad impression and ruin her chances forever. She was in panicky, fear-induced free fall.

In an effort to ease her fears, we made a pre-interview appointment so I could look over her resume and help her to prepare for the interview. Susan came to that appointment ten minutes late and very upset. She said that she had forgotten to bring her resume and was furious because she wanted me to look it over. She proceeded to recite a list of reasons why this had happened: drivers in the city were crazy, store clerks were incompetent . . . on and on she rambled. With each excuse, she took the blame off herself and placed it on an unjust, incompetent, and harsh world.

When she was done with her diatribe, I calmly looked at her and said: "Resistance. You 'forgot' your resume because your psychology *resisted* you remembering to bring it." She was in no mood to accept such an idea. "I just *forgot* it!" she exclaimed. "I planned on bringing it! I wanted to bring it! I printed out two copies, one for you and one for me so we could go over it together! What happened was . . ." And once again she proceeded to reiterate what she had just gone through, but this time with even more urgency and emotion. Unforeseeable things had happened. People had phoned unexpectedly. Her mother had asked her to pick up something from the store, but the cashier was new and didn't know how to work the computer. She had rushed home from her errands as quickly as she could, had showered, and had run out of her house only to arrive at my office ten minutes late—and empty-handed. "How could that be resistance?" she protested. "I want this job! It's perfect for me! Why would I resist bringing the resume when I really wanted you to see it?"

"Resistance," I repeated. "That's why you didn't bring it. It wasn't that you forgot to bring it. It's that you *resisted remembering.*" She wasn't convinced. She had too many good excuses. On and on we jousted, with her adamantly insisting that circumstances were responsible for her memory lapse and me calmly pointing out that it was her fear-driven defenses that were to blame.

At first glance, her reasons for forgetting the resume *were* convincing. Her day *had* been hectic. Her mother *had* asked her to pick up something from the store. City traffic *can* be bad. If you had heard about her day, you would most likely have had sympathy for her: "Poor baby! Of all days for this to happen! You've certainly had your share of bad luck!" For Susan, garnering sympathy from others was important, but it was even more crucial for her to be able to keep convincing herself that her excuses were always valid. She was bent on swaying the "jury" that resided in her psyche to find her "not guilty" of self-sabotage. And it understood. It forgave.

I, on the other hand, was not about to play along with her. I had an insider's view into her fears and insecurities. I knew how much change terrified her. I knew that deep down she felt like a fraud, and that she dreaded interviews in general and this one in particular.

I knew that it wasn't simple forgetfulness that had led her, one day before the most important interview she had had in years, to leave her resume at home. I suspected a more sinister culprit—the voice that kept screaming at her from the recesses of her mind, screaming that if I read her resume I would criticize it, screaming that she really didn't deserve such a great job, screaming that if she got the job she would fail at it, screaming that the interviewer would surely reject her and that she would be left humiliated and despondent. *That*

voice—not the traffic, not the phone calls, not the unexpected ob-
ligations and errands—was the reason why Susan had "forgotten"
her resume.

Once you accept the concepts outlined in this chapter, you can begin to take real control of your life. You can't fix a problem if you don't acknowledge that there's one to begin with, nor can you fix a problem if it's been wrongly diagnosed. In the following chapter, we'll look at specific strategies that will help you to move forward and make your dreams into realities.

take a moment...

1. List three things that you
haven't tried because you
were afraid that you would
fail. For each thing that you
list, complete the following
sentence: "If I failed at _____,
it would mean that I'm
_____." (Note: Reflect on
the validity of those answers,
and come up with other possible conclusions.)

15 It's as simple
as 1, 2, 3

The types of fears and insecurities that were outlined in the previous chapter can stop all forward in regard to the hopes, desires, and dreams of countless individuals. The damage is everywhere—people who once had great plans for their lives walk the planet with their heads down and shoulders hunched. They diligently work their nine-to-five job, come home, eat dinner, watch TV, and then go to sleep, only to start the same process again the next day. With little prompting, these people will regale you with all of their bad luck, bad breaks, and many disappointments: "If only I hadn't dropped out of . . .," "I know I could've done more except for that boss who . . .," "If I'd had a little more encouragement, nothing could've stopped me . . .," "I had responsibilities. What was I supposed to do . . . ?"

Have you settled into an uncomfortable and depressing life? Have you convinced yourself that living a life full of joy, creativity, passion, and fulfillment is unattainable and/or impractical? Certainly life's responsibilities demand attention. Bills are waiting to be paid and kids need to be fed. Reports need to be written, sales quotas met, shopping done, and friends called. "Fulfilling my innermost destiny?" you scoff. "Between fighting traffic, doing the dishes, and taking the clothes out of the dryer, if only I could find the time!" Have you ever seen an advertisement for a new product that you had actually thought of years ago? "I don't believe it!" you shout. "That was my idea!" The question you need to ask yourself is, why did someone else bring that idea to market and not you? What qualities did the product developer have that you didn't? What stopped you from moving forward?

One reason, I suspect, is that your automatic feelings and thoughts killed any real chance of your moving forward. If you don't give your insecurities and fears serious contemplation, they'll convince you how difficult it is to bring a new product to market or that your idea is silly or impracticable. Suppose one of your children came to you and said, "Hey, Dad! Hey, Mom! I've built this great new flying car for my toys to travel in!" Would you respond with, "You're just being silly. You need to be more practical"? Yet this is exactly what often happens. You become your own wet blanket for your creative, inventive thoughts. If your dreams are "impractical" . . . if they don't offer guaranteed success . . . if they aren't immune from ridicule, you'll label them as unreasonable or silly and relegate them to your dream "junk drawer." Somewhere along the line, you stopped asking for more from yourself and from the world, and became content to sit in the grandstand of life instead of playing in the actual game.

If your fears are powerful enough, they'll carve out a safe, bland life for you . . . a life where you're protected from taking any serious chances and risking any serious failures. But when we're unchallenged, we tend to drift intellectually, emotionally, and spiritually. Your fear-driven defenses, terrified of failure, keep you from stretching. Ever so slowly, it becomes easier and easier to give in to the low-grade depression that comes along with living a "shoulda" or "coulda" life, because, at the end of the day, depression is an appreciably better choice than following your dreams and failing to achieve them (which, according to the information that your fears rely on, you most assuredly would). Your fears are convinced that reaching for more will expose your flaws and bring you humiliation and shame.

A fragile psyche will do whatever's necessary to prevent further harm, even if the cost is a cardboard-cutout life. Imagine how different things would be if you were to release your fear-induced "emergency brake." Free of the shackles of self-doubt, you wouldn't move toward pragmatism so quickly. You would contemplate why and how things *could* work out instead of automatically believing that challenging yourself to stretch and grow would inevitably lead to failure and humiliation. You would challenge yourself to be better than you are. Transcending your fears would allow you to make a quantum leap forward in your personal evolution.

Your passions and dreams pose little threat to your insecurities as long as you allow them to remain only fanciful thoughts and musings that can easily be ignored or shooed away if you simply direct your mind to focus on other (more practical) things. Children will ask a parent to play only for so long. If they constantly hear, "We'll play as soon as I finish what I'm doing," they'll eventually stop asking. If you don't acknowledge and respect your dreams and desires and then take specific actions to achieve them, they'll become so discouraged at never being listened to that they'll slowly sink farther and farther into the recesses of your mind until they don't "bother" you anymore.

Bringing your ideas and dreams into the physical world is an essential first step toward achieving success and fulfillment. It represents your personal "Genesis"—your creation of your world. Martin Luther King "had a dream." How would the world have benefited if his dream had stayed only in his head? He transformed his dream into reality and brought it to bear upon an entire nation. We constantly take for granted the impact of the realized dreams of others. The cars you drive, the restaurants where you eat, the clothes you wear, the movies you watch . . . all of these things started out as ideas that someone was able to give form to. If these ideas had remained nothing more than mere thoughts, you would today be finding some other car to drive, another restaurant to enjoy, and a different outfit to wear! And, like the realized dreams of other people that you experience every day, the "silly" thoughts and dreams that burn in your heart are patiently waiting their turn ... if only you'll pay attention to them.

Even if you do find the courage to start making your dreams real, fears and insecurity can also lead you to lose focus. Have you ever sat down at your computer to start a project and suddenly been seized by an urge to clean house or to call an old friend? Did writing "Page 1" get postponed because you remembered that you had promised a friend that you would get together for a game of racquetball? Underestimating the impact of your fears is a common mistake that can lead to endless procrastination.

At what point did you become so fearful? Why do you have to be so careful? You're like a terrified child who's afraid to step into the street because a car might run you over. In fact, you're convinced that what lies around the corner is a speeding Mack truck loaded with rejection, failure, and humiliation.

Although failure is *a* possibility, it isn't the *only* possibility. Couldn't you just as easily find acceptance, success, and praise? Your challenge is to allow your dreams a chance to exist, to take them seriously, and to imagine their success before they're engulfed in a tsunami of "logic," practicality, and fear. There are millions of "wacky idea" success stories, but your fears will demand guarantees of success before you'll be allowed to move forward. This can create severe self-doubt and will stifle all momentum. Everything will stop.

One powerful first action you can take to counter your fears is to write down your ideas as soon as you have them. Writing things down on the spot transforms them because transferring thoughts into written words gives your heretofore ethereal ideas physical form. They become "things" that can be touched, looked at, and contemplated. Fleeting ideas that come and go as mood and time dictate turn into substantial three-dimensional entities, and, because they have that physical form, they become more difficult to dismiss and obliterate by something as easy as shifting your mental focus to something else.

The battle for personal fulfillment begins at your desk. Your first mission in this battle is to turn on your computer and put fingers to keyboard. It's a test of wills ... the will of the little boy or girl who lives in your unconscious and wants to protect you from failure, rejection, and humiliation battling the will of your adult self, which wants more from life than what you've arranged so far. Holding open the possibility that you can be successful will give you the psychological "capital" to move forward before your defensive "sledgehammer" pounds your hopes and dreams into oblivion.

> **The first step in challenging the messages of impending failure that your fears keep drilling into your consciousness is to force yourself to write down your desires, goals, projects, and ideas— regardless of how silly you may think they are.**

Here are some examples. When you have an idea for a product, give it a name, write that name on a piece of paper, and stick that paper on a bulletin board. Lo and behold, you've transformed yourself into a budding entrepreneur! When you have an idea for a play, give it a title and write it down. In so doing, you become an aspiring playwright! If you want to go back to school, have your transcripts sent to your chosen school and then set up an appointment with its educational advisor. Now you've become a prospective student!

Small, digestible steps are key to your idea gaining traction and creating momentum. If I always dreamed of opening a small café, here are the small (not overwhelming) steps I can take to move forward:

1. Write it down.

2. Find an area where I would want to open my restaurant.

3. Determine approximately how many square feet I would need.

4. Find out how much the rent is per square foot.

5. Determine how many seats the restaurant could hold.

6. Learn about the restaurant business by contacting local restaurant associations and culinary schools and researching information on the Internet.

7. Start working on a menu.

8. Determine my fixed and variable costs.

9. Determine how many customers a day I would need to average to break even and eventually turn a profit.

I can do all of these things in my spare time—even with a full-time job and a full life. If I give myself a year to study and plan, I eliminate the internal pressure of expecting instant success. I don't need to spend any money or sign any contracts. In the beginning my only goal is to educate myself so I can take a rational look at the feasibility of my opening a café. In the beginning, my only goal is to educate myself. After a year's worth of work, the next step I take—whatever it turns out to be—will not be nearly as intimidating as the fear that washed over me when the idea first came to me.

The concrete behaviors that you engage in today will change you the moment you make them. Your actions will become badges of self-respect, a respect that comes from the fact that you're not shutting yourself down and stopping all forward movement. Before other people and the world can take you seriously, *you* must first take yourself seriously. It isn't my intent to make light of your fears. They exist for a reason. They aren't evil. On the contrary, their only purpose is to protect you from harm. They see themselves as your protectors.

Remember Susan's fears in the previous chapter? They weren't trying to sabotage her chances of getting a job—they were only trying to protect her from humiliation and rejection. Her defenses took over the role of advisor. They whispered quietly into her ear: "It's not a good idea to take this interview. Stay where you are. It's too risky a venture."

Her defenses remembered all too clearly the consequences she had endured whenever she had stepped out in the past. They remembered the criticisms and second-guessing that her father had heaped on her. They remembered the taunts from cruel classmates who made fun of her when she was a shy and awkward adolescent. Her defenses were created to keep her from ever being placed in a position where she would be judged harshly again. That was their *raison d'être*. They worked hard to keep her safe, and safe she was going to be. If her defenses had their way, Susan would stay in her safe, depressing family job forever. They would never go along with her dream of getting into the "cockamamie movie business."

Susan hadn't "forgotten" her resume. She hadn't been the victim of a demanding and incompetent world that had conspired to have her leave her resume at home. If I had told her that she would be paid ten thousand dollars if she arrived at our session on time and with her resume, she would have arrived thirty minutes early, resume in hand. She would have made five copies and placed one in her purse and one in her car the night before.

No, Susan hadn't forgotten to bring her resume . . . she had resisted remembering. This may sound like a subtle distinction, but it has profound implications. The former holds "life" responsible. It follows the credo of "shit happens," which is exactly what you get when you allow yourself to be passive. To say that Susan "resisted remembering" puts responsibility back where it belongs—in this case, on her. It says that she's responsible for what happens in her life. It's your approach to life—whether you choose to remain a spectator or to become an active participant—that will determine whether your dreams become realized, or not.

take a moment...

1. List one or two things you've always wanted to do but have never "gotten around to." Some examples: I want to travel to China, I should join a gym, I should read more.

   a. Write down your rationalizations for not having done these things.

   b. Do these rationalizations hold merit? If not, what is your anxiety about behaving in ways that would contradict your rationalizations?

It's not as
easy as it seems

You now have a lot of tools at your disposal. You're excited and motivated to get started, but there are still some trap doors that you need to be aware of. For one thing, it can be unnerving to actually take the specific steps that real change requires. The feeling that washes over you may remind you of how you felt when you were ten years old and finally decided to dive off the ten-meter diving board at summer camp. Remember doing all the work to put yourself in a position to make the perfect dive, and then looking down, down, down into the shimmering water? Terror crept in and eventually took over. All of a sudden, completing the dive wasn't what was going through your mind. . . .

So here you are again, ruminating about the prospect of failure . . . of crashing into the hard, unforgiving water while making a fool of yourself. Silently you start to reevaluate your options—you can dive into (what you're convinced will be) pain and humiliation, or you can quietly creep back down the ladder and into the comfort of your chaise lounge.

Real change is hard. How many years have you been promising yourself that you would work out more or cut down on how much television you watch? How many promotions have you lost because you haven't kept up with your education? You scream at your children even though you promised yourself that you would find a better way to communicate with them. And weren't you supposed to reach out to your friends more often? And what about that photography class that you promised yourself you were going to take? In short, how many of your attempts at self-improvement have been derailed by "circumstances"?

Monitor yourself to determine if the things that irritate you in the people around you are actually things that may exist within yourself:

- You encourage your friend to tell her boyfriend that she resents him for not taking her on an exotic business trip—while you remain silent about having to spend every Thanksgiving with your spouse's family.

- You tell your brother to take a class at night to advance his career—while you sit home and watch hour after hour of television.

- You complain that your spouse never touches you—while in the bedroom you give off vibes that shout "Stay away!"

Pay attention to feelings of extreme anger or disgust that well up in you when you see certain behaviors in others. Extreme reactions can be seen as clues to unfinished issues that remain alive and well in your unconscious. Unconscious and unresolved issues can compel you to keep insisting to yourself and to others that you don't possess the very qualities that you're judging others for possessing. For example, if a man feels hatred for homosexuals and joins antigay groups, he would do well to examine why he focuses so much on something that leads him to spend so much time and energy on the very thing that he insists repels him.

Humans are complex. Your psyche is so powerful and so vast that you can engage in behaviors that are at exact cross-purposes simultaneously. It's like trying to climb to the top of a mountain while at the same time chaining yourself to a tree at its bottom. You reach for excellence while sabotaging your efforts at improvement.

Take notice of your conflicting feelings and behaviors. For example, I want to appear confident when speaking to a woman, yet I'm unable to make eye contact. This deficit is one I won't be able to work through because I'm not even aware that I'm not making eye contact. If I was aware of my fear and how it affected where my gaze landed, I would be able do something about it. I could consciously muscle through my desire to look away, or I could acknowledge how nervous I was by saying something like, "Gee, it's funny, but I'm a little nervous speaking with you. I guess I get a little jittery when I talk to an attractive woman." In this way, I would be able to present myself as a genuine person instead of as someone who was trying to manipulate or control an uncomfortable situation. By accessing my adult "I," I can deal with my feelings instead of letting my feelings deal with me.

This is "Awareness" with a capital "A." When you're angry, you're also aware, in the moment, of the full complexities of your anger. You're aware of what triggered it, and you're able to make connections to past event(s) that may be contributing to your current anger. In addition, you're aware of how the past may be affecting your perception of the present. Similarly, when you're afraid, you're also aware of the complexities of your fear, and so forth. When you're anxious, you're aware of the complexities of your anxiety, and so forth.

No one ever said this was going to be easy! But the key to accomplishing this level of awareness is to become reflective and contemplative—to question and then to seek out the reasons why you think and feel the way you do about individuals and events as they pass through your mind, heart, and life. It's particularly important to do this when you experience especially strong reactions to something. Whenever you feel afraid, disgusted, anxious, fearful, sad, or angry about a situation and or a person, it may be helpful to examine the full complexities of your feelings and reactions. Does the intensity of your feelings really match the situation at hand? When you deepen your self-awareness, you'll move away from reactivity and toward thoughtfulness and introspection.

take a moment...

1. Can you identify two or three "faults" or qualities in people or situations that trigger particularly strong reactions in you?

2. Can you match these reactions with qualities in yourself? For example: "I hate panhandlers" might match up to your feeling ashamed or humiliated about having had to ask your parents for help in paying your bills.

_____

_____

_____

_____

_____

_____

_____

_____

_____

_____

_____

_____

_____

_____

_____

_____

_____

Be careful
what you ask for

As you travel on the path of self-awareness, your fearful "self" will fight your efforts because fear seeks confirmation. If you come to believe that past traumatic events are no longer pertinent to your present situation, then the rationale for your fear's existence will cease to exist. Unfortunately, your "fearful" self, locked in the time warp of "long ago," continues to believe that the defenses that it has erected are essential to your well-being (and even survival), and that they must continue to protect you. But a life that's run through a filter of fear will lead you to believe that the world is dangerous and hostile.

This type of mindset generates a defensive approach to life. You play to "not lose" as opposed to playing to win. You end up constantly defending yourself against internal and external swords that you're convinced are hanging over your head. The internal sword consists of your "self-story": "I'm a loser . . . a failure . . .," and so forth. The external sword consists of the attributes that you assign to the world: "My coworkers are back-stabbing ladder climbers . . . Men are salacious, lecherous pigs . . . Women are money-grubbing materialists . . . Friends will only stick around as long as you don't ask anything substantial of them . . ." Over time, seeing the world as a dangerous place and people as out to hurt you until proven otherwise can lead to a state of hypervigilance. Taken to the extreme, this stance can lead to paranoia, isolation, and prejudice.

On the other hand, it can be foolish and naïve to assume that everything and everyone is wonderful. The difference between possessing a healthy sense of caution and allowing your fear to overtake and control you can be quite fuzzy. Is it wise to trust others when you've had experiences that tell you to do the opposite? Brenda was in what she thought to be a happy, loving marriage—until she found out that her husband was sleeping with her best friend. Why should she ever trust again, especially after coming home to find the two people she trusted more than anyone making passionate love? The new guy she's dating is saying and doing all the right things but, then again, she's heard it all before.

The media offer us little to enhance our feelings of safety and trust. Reporters act like private detectives whose purpose is to gather troublesome information. They remind us of what a dangerous world we live in. Every tragedy that can possibly befall us is not only explored but plumbed to its depths. Legions of news reporters listen in on police frequencies, scour court records, and are constantly on the lookout for the next celebrity tragedy.

If you're not careful, your fears will sweep you into a whirlwind of suspicion and anxiety. You'll spend so much energy guarding against phantom threats that you'll lose sight of your real needs and wants. Instead of embracing the world with joy and wonder, fear can direct you to protect against dangers that may exist only in your mind. The price you pay for being "safe" is that safety becomes your goal and supplants your passionate desires and dreams.

> *The truth of the matter is that the world*
> *is your servant. It will give you exactly what*
> *you ask of it. You have power over the world*
> *instead of the other way around.*
> *It will bend to your will.*

The first book in the Old Testament, the Book of Genesis, recounts how God created the world by literally thinking something and then having that thought take physical form. You possess this same type of power, albeit in a less dramatic form. Even though you can't materialize a Mercedes or a bar of gold, or will away cancer, you're far from helpless. You aren't a "god" in the literal sense since you're subject to a world that can just as easily strike you down with a disease as make you wealthy. Nevertheless, you still wield the power to create your own future based on your present.

The idea of karma is similar. I believe that we get back—often in this lifetime and sometimes in the same day, hour, or moment—exactly what we put out in the world. If we see the world as dangerous, then the world will bring us dangerous people and events. If Jerry sees black people as inherently evil, he'll find himself surrounded by black people who are genuinely evil. If Vicki thinks that people are inherently vicious and untrustworthy, she'll undoubtedly find people who will confirm her fears. On the other hand, if Roberta sees people as inherently good, kind, and decent, she'll most certainly find herself surrounded by those types of people—white, black, and everything in between. In short, it's from your own "sphere of being," so to speak, that your own personal Genesis arises.

Because this chapter piggybacks on the previous one, you can see how your world molds itself around the "I" that you project onto it. Who you are—your sense of personhood—is like a machete that, over the days, weeks, months, and years of your life, will carve out the space within which your life will unfold. The sharpness of your "blade," the strength of your "arms" to swing at adversity, and where you choose to focus your energies will determine whether you move toward self-actualization—or not. Take Peter as an example. Peter projects a victim persona, and the compliant world provides him with powerful, dominating individuals and institutions that he feels controlled and victimized by. Carol, on the other hand, projects a persona of confidence and vigor, and the world provides her with individuals who respect and challenge her, along with surroundings that she uses to her advantage.

Isolated behaviors or feelings are not enough to create a personal Genesis. One act of kindness does not make a kind person, nor does one act of selfishness make one selfish. The world that you create reflects the totality of who you are—your "psychological substance," so to speak. Who are you when no one else is around? That is your true, dominant "I," the "you" from which your present will be molded.

Some people are unable to accept this idea. They refuse to believe that the way people respond to them reflects what they put out into the world. No, Tom, your boss isn't out to humiliate you just as your last boss did. It's *you* who asked for the relationship that you've gotten. No, Shelly, men aren't repulsed by you. It's just that you're so prepared for rejection that your natural joy and happiness get walled off, and consequently people, including men, stay away.

Accepting an outlook of personal responsibility for creating your world can be tremendously powerful. Living with this type of personal worldview is an integral part of self-confidence and optimism in yourself, in the people and structures in your life, and in your future. Contrary to your childhood feelings of omnipotence, you never did have the power to change the things that happened to you when you were young, nor were you responsible for the fact that they happened in the first place. It's essential that you understand that then was then, but now is now. The person you are today has more resources, insight, and intelligence than the person you were when you were helpless and small. Today you control your world in ways that were completely beyond your capabilities when you were a little boy or girl.

Today, you're the artist who's painting the landscape of your life. If you've been beaten down by past tragedies or are living an unexamined, defensive life in which fear determines your future, the landscape you paint will be one of grays and off-whites. On the other hand, if you challenge yourself to achieve more and better than what you were given, if you commit to putting your personal stamp on your life, if you make a stand by saying, "*I* own the power to mold the world to my will. *I* decide what I do and what I believe. *I* will no longer passively stand by as the world happens to me because now *I* happen to the world," then the landscape you paint will be one of passionate reds, brilliant yellows, and emotionally laden blues.

You may feel that this chapter sounds somewhat moralistic—"Be a good person and good things will happen to you; be a bad person and ... " Certainly, we've all experienced times when the exact opposite happened. The saying "No good deed goes unpunished" is often true. Nevertheless, most of the time the world will conform to your will. You *are* the architect of your life. In light of this, you must be careful what you ask for. Because, sooner or later, the world will surely oblige.

take a moment...

1. Has your worldview changed in the last ten years? For example, do you think that people are kinder? Or more hateful? Is the world more dangerous? Or safer?

2. What can you do differently that will help you to create the world that you desire?

18   Stay!

Although achieving Awareness is essential in initiating behavioral change, it's only a beginning step because very often, when you *are* able to engage in a new behavior, it doesn't stick around long enough to become a permanent part of your personality.

> **When you start making behavioral changes,**
> **it's critical that you become aware of the tendency**
> **to revert back to your old ways when you don't get**
> **the (immediate) desired results that you hope**
> **these changes will bring.**

It's very common for people to give up on their best intentions. When you start eating healthier, working out four times a week, and exhibiting self-restraint and a sincere desire to lose weight—and at the end of the first month you find that you've actually *gained* three pounds (not realizing that muscle is heavier than fat), it's understandable that, discouraged and hopeless, you'll revert back to television, pizza, and beer.

Ron planned a romantic weekend away in an effort to rekindle his sex life with his wife. He told her how beautiful she was and how much she turned him on, but when she expressed hurt because he had neglected to notice her new dress, all of his good intentions faded away and he reverted to a position of, "Fine . . . why even try? What's the use?"

> *Expecting the world to immediately respond to you differently just because you've tried on a new behavior is a recipe for disappointment and failure.*

Jeffrey was an excellent example of someone who learned this lesson all too well. He was exceptionally shy, so much so that at twenty-three he had never even asked a girl out on a date. Our work together centered on self-exploration and on rebuilding his damaged self-image. Eventually he felt strong enough to take specific steps to interact and to ask a woman on a date.

> **Step 1:** He joined a book club—a *huge* step! As I've mentioned previously, insight without action is worthless. Jeffrey took one action that challenged his fears and defenses.

Things actually started out well—as luck would have it, the group consisted of him and nine women. He found Becky interesting and cute, and became interested in her.

The next step was to ask her out. At this point, his defenses exerted their full influence in an effort to put a stop to such *reckless* behavior. His fears demanded to be heard and kept telling him:

- "She wouldn't be interested in me."

- "I'm not tall enough."

- "She didn't smile back when I smiled at her."

- "She might not be the right religion."

- "If she turns down my invitation, I'll feel too uncomfortable to stay in the group, but I want to keep on attending it."

I challenged each excuse by pointing out that the conclusions he was jumping to were based on fear and not on actual experience. After much "negotiating," we came up with a compromise: instead of asking her out on a formal date, he would ask her if she'd like to have coffee after one of the group meetings.

Step 2: He asked her to coffee.
The fact that he was able to do this represented a tremendous win. It was a direct challenge to his fears and insecurities.

In a perfect world, time would have stopped right then and there. He really didn't need to hear her answer. He could have left the encounter feeling great about having accomplished something that he had never been able to do: ask a girl out on a date. He could have built on that success and moved on to other things. He had challenged his defenses. He had talked to a girl. He had asked her to coffee!!!! Bravo, Jeffrey! Job well done!

Unfortunately, we don't live in a perfect world, and the answer he did receive was less than perfect, although not awful by any means. Becky replied that she couldn't accept his invitation because she had to finish a report that evening.

If only Becky had known what Jeffrey had put himself through to nerve himself to invite her out, even casually. But she had no way of knowing that it had taken him eight months of twice-weekly therapy sessions, thousands of dollars spent, and countless hours of contemplation and internal discussion for him to get the courage to ask her the seemingly innocuous question, "Would you like to have coffee?" She didn't realize that standing before her was a man who had been viciously criticized and humiliated by his mother. She didn't hear his voice cracking or see his hands shaking as he spoke to her. Perhaps if she had been aware of all these things, she would have taken twenty minutes out of her evening and had coffee with him. Unfortunately (though understandably) her awareness reached only as far as a man in her book group asking her out to coffee on an evening when she was too busy to go.

> **Step 3:** Retreat ... retreat ... retreat.
> Jeffrey was devastated. His all-too-familiar feelings of being unattractive and boring—in essence, a loser—came rushing back. It was like hearing an old song on the radio. Instantly all the memories and emotions of the first time he had heard that song came back and washed over him like a familiar breeze.

When he arrived at my office the next day, he was completely dejected. His old insecurities were in full bloom. He spent the better part of the hour lamenting how pathetic he was and how hopeless things were. He was angry with me for having encouraged him, and he was disappointed in himself for having failed. He wondered why he had even tried. Who in God's name did he think he was?

The more difficult the challenges you face, the harder it is to generate real, lasting change. When nothing—career, finances, family, friendship, or relationships—seems to be going right, you can feel as if you're living under six feet of manure. In spite of difficult circumstances, you've mustered the energy and intention to make a heartfelt attempt to better your situation. You've challenged your fears and insecurities and become proactive. You've taken a class, stopped drinking, joined a gym, started a diet, or, in Jeffrey's case, joined a book club. Unfortunately, however difficult and monumental these actions may seem to you in the moment, they represent only a six-inch step up from the six-foot pit you've been mired in for years or perhaps decades. Yes, they represent a tremendous personal victory—but, at the end of the day, you're still under five-and-a-half feet of manure! In fact, sometimes you end up feeling worse. In Jeffrey's case, he was so discouraged after his "rejection" that he ended up feeling even more hopeless than when he had started working with me. Mind you, Becky's excuse may have been completely legitimate. In fact, she might even have accepted his invitation if he had asked her again the following week. Unfortunately, he didn't stick around the book group long enough to find out.

What you must embrace is your *journey* of self-evolution—not your ultimate destination. When you challenge your resistance to change, you have to modify what you accept as a victory. If you view everything short of achieving your desired outcome as a "failure," then failure is what you'll most often get. On the other hand, if you define having been able to take *specific action* as a "victory," then your victory is by definition the action you took, regardless of its immediate result.

You can't expect to hit a home run the first time you step into the batter's box, especially if you've never played baseball. In fact, you would be lucky to put wood on the ball. On the other hand, summoning up the courage to put on a uniform, grab a bat, and face a pitcher who's throwing a baseball at ninety miles an hour is a pretty awesome accomplishment. At least you weren't sitting at home watching the game on television, or in the stands drinking a beer and screaming at other people who at least had the courage to try. Whether you strike out or not, you've tried your best. You've shown up.

Jeffrey was so focused on reading a judgment of himself into Becky's reply that he interpreted her "I can't because I have to finish a report" as meaning that he was a worthless loser. On the other hand, he would have interpreted a "Yes, I'd love to have coffee" as meaning that he was desirable, valuable, worthwhile, and so forth.

The problem is that, either way, he wouldn't have been able to feel good about all that he had in fact accomplished by just showing up and meeting the challenge of inviting her in the first place. If he had, he could have patted himself on the back for having asked her, period, instead of feeling devastated by her answer. That reprieve might have given him enough psychological space to realize that his worst fears hadn't come true. She hadn't laughed at him, nor had she run away in horror. Instead, she had smiled and given him what could have been a perfectly plausible explanation. Or maybe she wasn't interested in him, but she hadn't been disgusted either. The point is that Jeffrey had finally gotten off the bench and stepped into the batter's box—and that was his victory.

Conceptualizing growth as a step-by-step process allows you to realize that each step is taking you one step closer to where you ultimately want to be. By redefining "victory," you'll come to realize that change is possible. In fact, you may realize that there's a world where your dreams and reality will finally meet.

take a moment...

1. Identify your biggest fear. Is this fear connected to your present-day circumstances, or is your past continuing to impact how you see your world today?

_____

_____

_____

_____

_____

_____

_____

_____

_____

_____

_____

_____

_____

_____

_____

_____

chapter

Love means
never having to say "I'm sorry"

I marvel at our psychological senility. Are you someone who keeps bashing your head against the same brick wall over and over again? Do you go on feeling blindsided and genuinely hurt by people (Mom, Dad, lovers, or friends) even though you know that they've repeatedly treated you (and most assuredly will continue to treat you) in inconsiderate, aggressive, and unloving ways? Are you dumbstruck when selfish, mean-spirited, competitive, discounting, dismissive, and unaware individuals once again act in ways that are consistent with exactly who they are?

When Dorie got a job that represented a huge step up in terms of money and responsibility, she couldn't wait to tell her mother the good news. She had high expectations for how the conversation would go, even though her mother had discounted all of her past accomplishments and was an expert at finding the negative in any situation. As Dorie dialed her mother's number, she was filled with excitement, anticipating that this time she would get the praise and encouragement that she so desperately craved. Regardless of what her past history was screaming at her to remember (that her mother was her mother, just as "MacDonald's was MacDonald's), Dorie felt crushed when her mother's only comment was, "I can't believe they didn't include a new car with their offer."

Somehow, some way, Dorie performed a Jedi mind trick and convinced herself that the "mother she had always dreamed of" would miraculously appear, even though her actual mother had been remarkably consistent in her inability to approve and support her. Her mother had never liked the people Dorie dated, the clothes she wore, or the way she lived her life, so why should the fact that Dorie had gotten a new job suddenly transform her mother into someone she had so clearly and consistently demonstrated she was not?

If I had spoken with Dorie before she called her mom and had asked her to objectively think about how the conversation would go (based on reality, not on the results she was hoping for), she most assuredly would have scripted out a conversation that would've come pretty close to what eventually happened. Even though she possessed this knowledge all along, she managed to not know what she did know so incredibly well. This type of irrational hope reminds me of my Las Vegas personality—when I enter the casino, I hope that I'll win, even though I'm pretty sure I'm going to lose. In spite of what history is telling me, when I put money on the table and am holding the dice are in my hands, I manage to convince myself that "this time" things will go my way.

In personal relationships, and especially with a parent, the reason you're able to convince yourself that "this time things will be different" is because you aren't asking for all that much from them. You're not asking for a million dollars, or for your mother to throw a huge party to celebrate your every success. "I'm so proud of you, sweetie!" would do just fine. How hard is that? Any decent person, especially a mother, would or should provide that, wouldn't she?

But when you don't get your hoped-for response or reaction, a chain of events unfolds:

- You try to educate her: "Why can't you just say congratulations?"

- You roll your eyes in disbelief and wonder if she'll ever get a clue.

- You feel discouraged and depressed.

- You feel anger and rage about her lack of support.

Of course, all of the above responses seem reasonable. You have every right to challenge her, roll your eyes, or feel discouraged and/or angry. In fact, you'll use the certainty that you've been wronged as justification for your reactive behavior. Becoming agitated has the added benefit of diverting your attention so you don't have to explore the real meanings that underlie the hurtful statements being inflicted on you. If Dorie were able to closely examine the meanings behind her mother's response, she might hear something like this:

- "You're a disappointment to me. I don't have faith that you can and will succeed. This is why I automatically think that you'll fail and why I say the things I say," or

- "I'm threatened by your success. You're becoming everything I never was, and I can't stand to see you succeed where I've failed."

These hidden messages can be so hurtful that your unconscious desire to not decipher them is understandable. Your automatic reactions to these types of statements have the effect of pushing away their true meaning. You'll rant, yell, and lose sleep. You'll talk to friends for hours on end and complain bitterly while never looking (or, more likely, being too terrified to look) at what the underlying message really is.

Understanding Hidden Messages
Here are some advanced communication techniques that will help you to get to the core meanings of what the people in your life are telling you.

First, when confronted with disappointing responses or

behaviors, refrain from asking "Why?" questions such as "Why can't you?" or "Why did you?" Questions, or statements that lead to other (disappointing) responses, also often lead to more conflict. When you pose a question like "Why can't you just say ..." or "Don't you realize that ...," you won't get the result that you're hoping for because deep down you have the (irrational) hope that the answers you get will reflect caring, insight, and real understanding. Unfortunately, those answers will often be defensive and evasive:

> **The question:** "Why can't you just say con-gratulations?" leads to the answer: "You know I'm proud of you. Why, just last week I was bragging about you to ..."

> **The aggressive statement:** (not a question per se, but a response that often leads to the same type of defensive response, such as "You never say anything encouraging about my successes," leads to the response, in this case from Dorie's mother): "Nothing I say makes you happy. I only said what I said to help you."

And before you know it, you're in the middle of a debate about details, and you become intent on proving that the other person is wrong. Your goals change. In the beginning, you wanted to be loved, accepted, and understood, but the conversation quickly turns into a desperate effort on your part to try to convince the other person (Mom, Dad, partner, or friend) just how hurtful and illogical they're being.

One excellent way to uncover or expose underlying feelings is to refrain from asking defensive questions. Instead of having an automatic reaction, take a moment for thoughtfulness and reflection and, from this position, make self-reflective statements instead.

> *Making a statement about how you're feeling is a much more powerful way of communicating then asking a question about why others have said or done what they said or did. It leads to deep and profound conversations.*

If you turn a question into a statement that reflects your true (uncomfortable) feelings, it will sound something like:

"Do you still care about me?"

Self-reflective statement: "You feel distant to me. It seems as if your feelings have changed. I don't feel loved by you the way I used to."

—⟋⟍—

"Why don't you touch me any more?"

Self-reflective statement: "I don't think you find me sexy," or "I feel unattractive and undesirable around you lately."

—⟋⟍—

"Why do you always seem to find something wrong with everything I do?"

Self-reflective statement: "You have contempt for me," or "I feel as if I don't meet your expectations of what I should be."

—⟋⟍—

"Why don't you call me anymore?"

Self-reflective statement: "We've grown

apart and it's breaking my heart. I wonder if you still care."

—⟶⟵—

"Why don't you ever ask me about my life?"

Self-reflective statement: "You really aren't all that interested in me," or "I don't feel important to you."

—⟶⟵—

"Why can't you just say congratulations?"

Self-reflective statement: "I feel as if I'm a disappointment to you."

Statements like these instantly take communication to deeper levels because, by their nature, they direct conversations towards core issues. You want to move from being a water skier (cruising along on the surface) to becoming a scuba diver (taking communication to a deeper and more revealing place). A statement such as "Do you care?" takes a genuine feeling ("I'm hurt and scared") and moves it into an intellectual exercise. These types of "water-skiing" questions are aggressive in nature and will often put the other person on the defensive. The response you're apt to get is something along the lines of, "What do you mean 'Do I care?' Of course I care!" At this point, the other person will often follow up with his or her own (aggressive) question, such as: "Why would you ask such a ridiculous question?" And again, before you know it, you're in the middle of circular and dysfunctional argument.

You can also be effective in deepening communication when you're on the receiving end of such questions. For example, when someone asks, "Do you care?," you can give the simple answer, "Of course I care!," which will stop the conversation in its tracks—or you can chose to move toward a deeper level of communication. To do this, you'll need enough psychological reserves to resist the knee-jerk reaction to respond defensively ("Of course I care!"). The more you rely on the internal value of being inquisitive, and the more you commit to understanding others, the better you'll be able to respond nondefensively. For example:

"Do you care?"

Defensive reply: "Of course I care! I can't believe you keep asking me this question." (This reaction will shut down all communication or lead to a fight.)

Nondefensive reply: "It seems as if you have your doubts." (This reply is nondefensive because it leaves you open for more of the same types of questions or statements.)

As an aside, how many times have you had recycled fights regarding the same core issues, with different triggers and circumstances, over and over again? These could be with your parents, your lovers, or your friends, and they could be about money, sex, time spent together, old boyfriends or girlfriends who periodically call, and so forth. The reason why issues keep getting recycled is that when they come up, they're not dealt with well. The conversation usually gets shut down or diverted onto some other topic, only to pop up again on another occasion. Here's more extended example:

"I guess I have my doubts about whether or not you care."

Defensive reply: "You're always complaining about something. Nothing makes you happy." (This reply will put the person you are talking with on the defensive as he or she loses focus on the original issue.)

Nondefensive reply: "I'd like to hear them." (Once again, you're leaving yourself completely open and defenseless. You're asking to know more.)

—⁓—

"Well, you seem so wrapped up in that project you're working on. You just don't seem to be paying much attention to me anymore."

Defensive reply: "I can't believe how needy you are! And besides, I'm here right now, aren't I?" (This aggressive and we can see where this conversation will end.)

Nondefensive reply: "That must leave you feeling very alone." (A beautifully empathic response! This answer makes the other person feel truly cared for—the very thing he or she was complaining about in the first place!)

A key point here is that you aren't debating whether the complaint that the other person is trying to make is objectively valid or not. In your mind, you may care very much about that person. The project that you're working on may be exceptionally difficult, stressful, and boring, and the fact that you're working so hard has nothing to do with your emotional feelings toward the other person. But when you move away from automatic reactions, you give yourself the space to identify core issues. It's critical to remember that the original complaint is often only a stepping-stone toward deeper issues and feelings. Remember, process—that is, how you communicate and how you engage in conflict, is often more important than the objective fact(s)—i.e., "I do care."

> *A nondefensive communication style is reparative in and of itself. Very often, nothing more has to be done to ease the other's pain than to listen, in a very deep and caring way, to what the other person is saying. You don't have to try to convince the other that you care in response to a past event because you're showing that you care in the present moment—and in a very profound way!*

Defensive reply: "You make it sound like I enjoy working on that project. My God, all I do is bust my butt, and I still get no appreciation!"

This makes you the victim while the original issue gets pounded into submission (until it comes up three months later!). Eventually both parties tire of this useless exercise and the subject gets changed or one of you rolls over and goes to sleep.

Two other key elements of nondefensive communication are to refrain both from saying "I'm sorry" and from trying to fix the problem immediately. These strategies are usually ineffective and tend to shut down deeper communication.

Carol and William are at a party:

Carol: "I can't believe that you talked to that redhead for such a long time."

William: "She works for a company that does business with mine. I was just talking shop with her."

This explanation, if true and said with care and sincerity, should defuse the situation. If it doesn't, something else is most likely in play.

> **Carol:** "Well, it just seems as if you were having way too good a time with her."

> **William:** "Look, I'm sorry. I didn't mean to ignore you."

An apology, especially a quick apology, is often code for this very different message: "If I apologize, will you shut up? Can't we talk about something else?"

> *When you know that you're in the wrong, or if you want a conversation to end, you think (or rather hope) that an apology will satisfy your partner and end the discussion. However, this strategy often fails because saying "I'm sorry" is often meant as (or taken as) an unspoken code for what you really mean to say—which is: "Shut up!"*

Experience should tell you that these kinds of "apologies" rarely work. They may placate the offended person in the moment, but they do nothing to process deeper feelings of anger, insecurity, or abandonment.

When an apology fails to defuse a situation, which is most often the case, you may resort to trying to incorporate a "fix." In this example, William has said that he's sorry that he talked with the redhead, but Carol is still upset. So he takes the next step and goes into "fixing" mode:

> **William:** "Fine. I'll tell you what—I'll never talk to another woman without getting your approval first."

This statement is code for: "If I do that, will you shut up and leave me alone?"

—\\\\—

Carol: "You know that's not what I mean. It just seemed that you liked her."

William: "Liked her? I hardly know her! You know I love you! You're the only one for me! Now stop being so silly, and let's get something to eat."

This reply is code for: "If I tell you I love you, will you finally shut up and leave me alone?"

> *Saying something like "Fine, you're right" or "I'll never talk to her again" is a code for not saying what you would really like to say, which is, "What do I have to do to get you to shut up?"*

Although it's nice of William to remind Carol that he loves her, mouthing platitudes rarely takes the conversation into deeper feelings of insecurity or trust. Unresolved issues have a habit of resurfacing in different situations with different triggers—for example, if William should smile at the supermarket checkout clerk, look in the direction of a pretty girl while he and Carole are having dinner at a restaurant, or mentions the bright new employee who's been hired at his office.

Let's assume that William's conversation with the redhead was exactly as he described it—only shoptalk, with no inappropriate feelings or behaviors. Since his initial explanation did not defuse the situation, there's an excellent possibility that something deeper is going on with Carol. Her *real* upset may have nothing to do with William's party conversation. Her reaction may be due to a difficult parental relationship, or it could be based on an earlier romantic relationship in which her trust was violated. William will never learn about the complexities of Carol's core issues unless he fully commits to employing communication techniques that will lead him to understand them.

Another dysfunctional communication technique is to use logic as a way of maneuvering out of uncomfortable situations. This happens when you try to convince others that they're wrong, insecure, paranoid, overbearing, dependent, or hysterical. If you succeed, you hope that you'll get them to admit that they're wrong for having their feelings and that somehow they'll then "delete" their upset from their consciousness. The problem is that people, whether "wrong" or not, still have their feelings, and all you'll accomplish by "outsmarting" them is shaming them for having their feelings in the first place.

If you "lawyer" others enough, they'll never want to come to you with their uncomfortable feelings. Your lovers, children, parents, or friends will begin to feel that they have to be absolutely "right" in order to be allowed to express any of their true feelings. Over time, they'll stop seeing you as someone they feel safe with because they fear that they have to hide their insecurities or risk your discounting or dismissing them.

> *A high form of love occurs when you don't shame others when they present their most vulnerable selves to you. Committing yourself to understanding as opposed to defending or counterattacking is the key to this process.*

Another key communication technique is to *have one conversation at a time*. This means that you commit to understanding others without concern for having your point of view being heard. You make the selfless decision that for the time being you'll empty your mind of all the things that you want to say in response to the feelings (anger, accusations, and so forth) that those others are expressing. This represents a commitment to understand, on a very deep level, others' thoughts and feelings. Period. You need to trust that you'll have ample time to express your own feelings later, but in the moment, your goal becomes to have others feel truly heard, even (or especially) if you're convinced that they're wrong.

You know how frustrating it is when people you're arguing with aren't listening to what you're saying. Instead, they're thinking ahead about what their point is and how they're going to make it. You're afraid to stop talking because you know that as soon as you do your "opponents" will instantly jump all over what you've said and bombard you with their version of how things *really* are. Things quickly turn into contests of who's right and who's wrong:

> **Felicia:** "I can't believe how you never listen to me."
>
> **Ray:** "What're you talking about? This entire relationship is about you!"

Here we have two valid complaints that deserve airing. However, nothing will get solved if these issues are discussed at the same time. If Ray could commit to exploring how it is for Felicia to feel as if he never listens to her (which would entail his *really* listening to her, and hence offering a reparative experience in the moment), she might be willing to listen to him (at a later time) about his comment that the relationship is entirely about her (which, if she really focused in on him, would stop being about her and would be reparative as well!).

When you react automatically, you rob yourself of the opportunity to learn. It's as if someone were to tell me, "Gary, your fly's undone," and I immediately responded with, "Well, your shoes are untied!" In other words, ridiculous.

Suppose Gail says: "I can't believe how you acted last night at Bob's party. You were obnoxious and overbearing!" If I'm coming from a nondefensive place, I'll try to find out what her view of things was by responding: "Well, I know that I can be obnoxious and also overbearing. What makes you say this in regards to Bob's party?" Gail then explains: "You went on and on about that project you're working on. You interrupted Natalie twice, and you were talking really loudly."

There's an old Buddhist saying: "You can't see your own eyebrows." When your loved ones critique you, look at it as a gift that can offer you insights into yourself. By being nonreactive, I can evaluate Gail's criticism. If I determine that it's valid, I can own up to it: "You know, I think you may have a point. Bob's so good-looking and so successful that I was probably trying to impress him. I didn't realize that I was coming across so poorly. I think I may have some fence-mending to do." On the other hand, if I didn't agree with her, I could say something like: "I can understand why you may think that, but, upon reflection, I was really excited about the project. I was talking loudly because I was passionate and excited." If I wanted to delve deeper, I might ask Gail why she got so triggered. Perhaps this had more to do with her than with me. But either way, the conversation will constructive rather than destructive.

The best way to be heard is to listen well.

When people feel truly understood, they don't feel the need to repeat things over and over again (how many times have we screamed, "You've said that ten times already!"?). It's calming to feel cared for and understood, and when this happens, conflict often relaxes into a conversation.

It's important to remember that you can use the techniques I've outlined in this chapter in all types of interactions, not just between lovers. Communicating on a high level will advance your conversations with friends, family members, coworkers, customers . . . basically every relationship and interaction you have. High-level communication is a reflection of your emotional evolution

> **The pathway to loving relationships is found through communicating on a deep and meaningful level. How you communicate your feelings is a testament to how you love.**

Committing to trying to truly understand those you're with is deeply loving. It's incredibly loving and courageous to say: "I can see that you're injured by something I said or did. I really want to know more about what you're experiencing and feeling." In essence you're saying, "Tell me your feelings about how you feel that I disappointed you."

This is a selfless act. In the service of understanding others and easing their pain, you're actually inviting further criticisms. You're showing that you're willing to face your own uncomfortable issues. It means that you value the other more than you value your pride or your need to be right. This kind of communicative *process* is deeply loving and healing. There's no need to shut others up, to outthink them, or to divert their attention onto something else. You don't need to stop difficult conversations—in fact, you welcome them. You want to hear *more* because you're committed to understanding those you're with. Love truly means never having to say "I'm sorry."

take a moment...

1. Think of some questions that you recently asked someone as a way to avoid what you were really feeling and really wanted to say.

2. What were the feelings you had that underlay those questions?

3. Think back to the most recent fight you had with someone close to you (husband, wife, sibling, parent, friend). Try to identify the two conversations that were taking place simultaneously.

I think

I'll have . . .

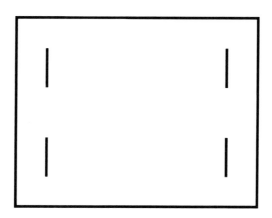

Okay, here's your challenge: intersect the four vertical lines in the square by using two straight lines that are connected at either end. In other words, the two lines that you use to intersect the four lines must be configured to look something like this:

Any luck? The puzzle is solvable, but if you haven't figured it out after a few minutes, chances are you won't be able to. And what will prevent you from solving it are certain assumptions you've made that place limits on how you approach it and that make this entirely solvable (and actually easy) puzzle infuriatingly difficult. If you could allow yourself to conceptualize the problem differently, you would solve it in seconds.

Here's the solution:

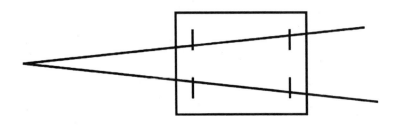

Have you ever heard the expression, "Think outside the box"? Well, if you didn't solve this puzzle, it's because you stayed inside the box. Where did I say that you had to do that? You *assumed* that you had to when *no such restriction was stated*, but once you made this assumption, solving the puzzle became impossible. It's these types of internal limitations that prevent you from solving not just this puzzle, but many of life's puzzles as well. You exert a great deal of energy to better your life, yet you still have trouble getting out of the mess you're in, so you throw up your hands, convinced that there's no possible solution. Like Susan in Chapter Fourteen, you become a "Yes, but ..." person who comes up with multiple reasons why you can't go outside the box.

Ashley's a good example of someone who made her "box" as small as possible. If a negative perspective about a situation existed, she would find it. She raced toward victimhood as if she were late for a bus. While it's true that a troubled childhood had left her with much to be bereft about, her method of dealing with past traumas was to create turmoil in the present. In an attempt to recreate and rectify her past (over which she had no power or control), she would create turmoil and then attempt to control it.

One day she was telling me how much she hated her birthdays. She complained that she didn't have a boyfriend, that she was getting older, that she wasn't as far along in her career as she had hoped to be, that her father was a jerk, that her car was acting up, that traffic was bad, and that her boss was mean. Her pity party was in full swing.

No doubt you've heard the term "learned helplessness." In Ashley's case, "learned misery" was more appropriate. Her worldview put her in a constant position of need.

Still, there's something very seductive about "pity partyers" because it's easy for you to become a hero. You can confidently reassure them that things will turn out all right and then embark on rescuing them—which is relatively easy because the people you're saving from drowning are often in water that's only three feet deep!

What Ashley failed to realize was that the miseries she complained about so bitterly were actually choices she had made. For example, regarding her angst about her birthdays, the specific circumstances (lack of a boyfriend, and so forth) surrounding each particular birthday didn't determine in advance that the day would turn out to be miserable.

Ashley's decision to have a lousy birthday was an attempt to stave off the possibility of being disappointed if she expected to have a great birthday only to have a miserable one. So she *decided* in advance that she would have a miserable one. In her view, it was better to know that she was going to have a bad time than to hope for a great day and then be bitterly disappointed.

However, although Ashley made a decision to be miserable, she also had the ability to make a decision for joy. The option of having a great birthday certainly existed, and all she had to do was choose it. She could have committed herself to greeting her birthday with a big smile, to making plans for dinner with her friends or family, or both, and to do something fun, extravagant, and exciting.

Here's another example. Suppose I learn that my plane is late and that I'm going to miss my connecting flight. I can respond to this news in many ways. Some obvious ones are to feel disgusted, angry, frustrated, miserable, or outraged. I can yell at the airline staff, curse under my breath, and complain about the incompetence of the airline industry to anyone who'll listen.

However, another approach I could take would be to choose to use the extra time to catch up on some reading, to explore a new city (since I have to stay there overnight), or to take a much-needed nap. I can choose to view the current situation with a sense of perspective and wisdom—that what's done is done, and there's nothing I can do about it, so I might as well make the best of a difficult and inconvenient situation.

Experience will tell you that most days contain within them a certain amount of pain, discomfort, and disappointment ...

- Bank tellers will be incompetent.

- Traffic will be gridlocked.

- People will be unkind, inconsiderate, and downright rude.

- Business plans will be delayed or altered.

- Other people will get credit for work that you did.

- Less qualified workers will be promoted before you are.

- Car tires will go flat and car batteries will die.

- Feelings will get hurt.

- Sincerity will be misunderstood for rejection.

- And, inevitably, right after you pick up your freshly washed car, a bird will crap on it!

If you accept the premise that the world will be difficult, and sometimes *very* difficult, you can also, as of this moment, decide in advance what responses you will choose when these yet-to-happen nuisances arise.

The ability to make more evolved choices depends on whether you possess strong internal values—or not. It is these values that will inoculate you against losing your psychological balance, since core values are not wedded to external circumstances. Internal values reflect your best and most highly evolved self, and will bring order to a chaotic and often uncaring world. By definition, they are unchanging and unaffected by external circumstances.

You *can* decide to be guided by your internal values regardless of whether good or bad comes your way. You *do* have the ability to choose:

To stop reacting . . .
To stop being shocked when bad things happen . . .
To stop whining . . .
To stop complaining . . .
And to stop, think, and promise yourself that you'll no longer become predictably miserable, angry, depressed, irritable, hopeless, and helpless because of the disappointments that arise in any ordinary day, week, month, year, or lifetime.
Instead, you can choose to opt for more from yourself and for personal excellence.

Some people jump at the chance to complain about how badly they have it, or, in other words, to whine about their lot in life. A whine is when you identify a problem without thinking of a solution. Here are some common whines:

- "I hate my job."

- "My boyfriend always yells at me."

- "I hate living in this city."

- "I don't have any friends."

- "I can't meet my boss's expectations."

- "No one listens to me."

- "I can't lose weight."

- "I never have enough money."

While things may be difficult, where are the solutions? Is "I hate my job" end of story? You're certainly allowed to complain. In fact, you may take great advantage of this right now— but at the end of the day, what are you going to do about your problem? "I hate my job, so I'm going to night school to advance my career" isn't a whine. It's a statement of intent . . . a statement of purpose. "No one listens to me, so I'm going to become a better listener so I can better understand other people"—again, not a whine but a demonstration of courage and determination.

Choices abound. You just need to quiet your defenses long enough to access them.

No doubt life is difficult, but there's a lot more that you can do about your difficulties than just telling yourself, and everyone else, how miserable things are. You have the option of choosing personal excellence in the face of mediocrity, dysfunction, and adversity. You can:

- **Choose** in advance to not feel terrible when your

parent continues to act in disapproving and rejecting ways.

* **Choose** to let a car into your lane and not to
become enraged at traffic or at other drivers'
idiosyncratic driving behavior.

* **Choose** to be understanding when you encounter clerks or salespeople who are slow, underqual-
ified, or simply having a bad day.

* **Choose** to turn off the television and pick up a
good book when you get home from work.

* **Choose** to praise your subordinates for their
positive accomplishments rather than only pointing out their faults.

* **Choose** to not take other people's rudeness or
selfishness personally.

* **Choose** to have a great day and to make a con-
certed effort to find good in every situation.

Suppose that your boss is mean to you even though you've
made many efforts to please, understand, and placate her. If
you need (or want) to continue working where you are, at
least for the foreseeable future, what are your options? One
option is to let circumstances dictate your mood and behavior.
In other words, you can go into work with a (justifiably) bad
attitude, mutter under your breath, and curse your luck at being stuck in such a rotten place. However, another option is
to rely on solid internal values that will allow you to maintain
your standards regardless of your having to work under a difficult person.

With strong internal values, your desire for excellence, dig-
nity, and integrity will shine through. These values don't come

and go as external circumstances dictate. If they're values that you truly hold dear, then they'll certainly stand firm in the face of something as relatively insignificant as a boorish or even hateful boss.

> **Relying on internal values allows you to go outside the "box" of your circumstances (such as a jerk for a boss).**

When you're able to transcend situational constraints, you'll find that you're free to come from *your best self.* You can choose to live with excellence regardless of your environment. The values of integrity and excellence will propel you to give one hundred percent regardless of whether your efforts are appreciated or not. When you do this over time, your company, your coworkers, and your customers are bound to be impressed with your work ethic. If your boss is unable to see your value, that will be a reflection on her—not on you.

I can already hear you protesting: "Gary, you don't understand *my* boss! This guy is such a pig! All he does is criticize and humiliate! And the customers—forget it! They're demanding, rude, and obnoxious! If you think it's so easy, then *you* deal with them!" Of course, you're right. I don't know your problems. What's also true is that your problems are *yours.* They're not mine. You're the one who's stuck in your miserable situation. The question that must be answered is: what are you going to do about it? What internal values are you going to access when your boss acts without insight and care? Tomorrow you're still going to go back to the same jerk of a boss and to the same disgusting customers. Are you telling me that you have no other options except to whine? That because of external circumstances, *you must* become unhappy, unprofessional, withholding, and miserable? *You have choices.* The problem is that you don't like your choices, which are:

A. To do nothing: This is pretty much self-explanatory. You accept your powerlessness to change your situation and you suffer in silence or complain just for the sake of complaining.

B. To react to your circumstances by becoming angry, vindictive, withholding, and retaliatory.

C. To identify core values that will guide you regardless of the difficulty of the external circumstances that you may face.

Choice C is a not an easy choice because in the (often difficult) moment it doesn't alleviate the problems you're facing. Committing to be the best employee you can be may do nothing to change your sadistic boss. In addition, some people may interpret your seemingly conciliatory behavior to mean that you're a pushover who can be easily manipulated.

Because choice C often offers delayed and ambiguous rewards, it's frequently ignored in favor of A or B. In Chapter Eighteen, I gave the example of being under six feet of manure and, after doing something proactive, moving up only six inches. You may reason that this is unacceptable and come to the rational conclusion that it's just not worth doing. This, for example, is why diets so often don't work. When overweight people commit to eating better and to working out at the gym four times a week but find after a month of suffering that they've lost only seven pounds, they may reasonably think: "What's the win in going from three hundred and fifty to three hundred and forty-three pounds? I'm still a big fatso! Forget it! Why order plain pasta with vegetables and olive oil? I'll have the pasta alfredo!"

If you're strictly results-driven, you'll want a guarantee that if you make the herculean effort to change, then joy, bliss, and success will surely follow. However, this kind of approach leaves you with two very limited options:

A. Keep things exactly the same.

B. Try something new, but only with a guarantee that joy and success will follow immediately.

Given the fact that option B is highly unlikely, option A is seen as the better choice.

Striving for excellence sounds nice on paper, but walking that walk is often exceptionally difficult. In my work as a management consultant, one of the most common complaints I hear from employees is that even though they may do fifty things right, the only time they hear from their supervisor is when they do something wrong. This is tremendously discouraging. What is someone to do when this happens repeatedly?

Aside from getting a new job or moving to a different department, the one thing you can do is to make performing with excellence a personal goal. I don't mean to excuse the unenlightened and often mean-spirited behavior of some people, but if your commitment to excellence lasts only as long as the praise you receive for it, then your commitment to praise is greater than your commitment to excellence. This may sound unsympathetic, but it isn't intended to be. The goal is to embrace your commitment to excellence and to let it be your guide instead of having it fade away when you find yourself confronted with an intimidating, aggressive manager.

Have you ever worked with colleagues who acted busy whenever the supervisor was nearby and then shut things down the moment "the coast was clear"? What these types of people fail to realize is that their work habits demonstrate to all those around them what kind of people they really are. Coworkers may be amused at the shenanigans, but deep down they don't admire their colleagues' shirking, or their manipulation of the boss. They see workers like this in all their ignominious splendor. And when these coworkers get promoted, they'll be sure *not* to bring shirkers along because they've seen firsthand what kinds of workers they *really* are. Imagine how differently these coworkers would evaluate their colleagues if they knew them to be diligent, joyful, helpful, and committed to excellence—even in the shadow of a harsh, critical boss.

Every day, with every life experience, we're surrounded by realities, both present and past, real and imagined, that can serve as reasons for us to give up before we begin. *Anything* can become a reason to retreat into mediocrity:

- Girls won't talk to you because you don't drive a nice enough car.

- Guys ignore you because you're not pretty enough.

- Your parents never offered you encouragement and criticized all of your decisions. Your friends are better looking than you, and their families have more money and better business connections.

- You're fat, black, short, bald, or _____, and people discriminate against you because of it.

- You were molested as a child and can't shake the shame, fear, and anger that cling to you.

- Your older brother (or sister) was your parent's favorite, so he (or she) is the one who's supposed to succeed.

- You're addicted to drugs or alcohol.

- You never had a chance to go to the right school.

- You have too many responsibilities now—you're stuck where you are.

- Your boss is overbearing.

- Your coworkers are backstabbers.

Certainly the world is full of inequalities but, at every moment, each of us is equal in how we respond to our world.
Every moment of every day, we are free as to what type of
choices we make. When two people arrive back home at the
end of their workday, they're equal. It doesn't matter that one
drives a fifteen-year- old clunker while the other has a new
Mercedes. It doesn't matter that one lives in a one-bedroom
apartment while the other has a palatial mansion. Nor does it
matter that one had a great childhood and the other a tragic
one. Between the time they get home and the time they go to
bed, they're both equal in their ability to make choices. They
could:

- Open up and drink the first of six beers (or glasses
  of wine, or cognac).

- Greet their children with a hug and a kiss and then
  engage them in a detailed conversation about their
  day.

- Turn on the television and watch it for the next
  four hours.

- Get ready to go to the gym.

- Go online and stay in chat rooms until bedtime.

- Read a book.

- Spend time on a hobby.

- Take a walk with a friend or a family member.

- Get stoned.

- Finish the report that's overdue.

- Research night schools that offer MBAs.

- Molest their daughter.

- Call their son an idiot.

- Gather the family around the dinner table and engage in a lively discussion.

- Start writing a play.

- Meditate.

- Learn a new computer program.

- Sculpt.

- Watch the ball game while ignoring their spouse and children.

- Eat a huge dinner and then a pint of ice cream.

- Write up a business plan for a product they've been thinking about.

- Organize an employee softball or bowling league.

- Join a political organization.

Neither the obstacles that presently stand in your way nor the difficulties that you've experienced in the past can *force* you to make a particular choice. Every time you open the door to your home and walk inside, you have options. No one's forcing you to open that can of beer, to turn on the television, or to spend the next four hours vegetating.

When it comes right down to it, you're faced with three choices:

- Excellence

- Mediocrity

- Failure

Excellence is the option that carries with it the most difficulty because it requires a direct challenge to your fears and insecurities. Mediocrity and failure will take care of themselves with little or no effort on your part (although you may use your resources to help the process along!). Laziness (otherwise known as "resistance to effort") will move you toward mediocrity or failure.

Excellence and passivity cannot coexist. Excellence requires action because, without action, thoughts of real achievement quickly turn into nothing more than the blathering of "wannabees." A lot of people talk a great talk. They expound on their high-minded ideas about what to do to make the world a better place. They talk about how rotten the political system is and what should be done to better it. They'll spend hours pontificating on any and all subjects, but when all the air has left their diaphragms, they will do absolutely nothing concrete to bring their ideas into existence. These people speak in terms of "if only," "should have," "could have," or "when this happens, I'll be able to ..." The problem with thinking about what "should" happen is that you never get to the place of "I'm going to." Thinking "great thoughts" can delude you into believing that you're taking giant steps toward excellence when, in reality, all you're doing is going round in circles.

> *Intent is the key. Saying things like*
> *"I need to . . . "*
> *"I'm going to . . ."*
> *"I want to . . . "*
> *"I should . . . "*
> *"I could . . . "*
> *medicates you into believing that you're really moving*
> *forward. Changing "I want to . . ." to "I intend to . . . "*
> *represents a powerful change in how you see and*
> *present yourself to the world and to yourself.*

Excellence, by definition, is rare. That's why it stands out and why the world responds so favorably to it. Imagine a clerk at your local convenience store greeting you with a big smile.

He asks how your day is going and offers to help you find something. When you leave with your cup of coffee and dough-nut, he says, "Have a great day! See you next time!" Surely this clerk could justify wallowing in the misery of working at a bor-ing job for minimum wage. On the other hand, he could also make the choice to embrace excellence as his guiding light and to live his life accordingly.

Some people feel that approaching mundane or difficult re-lationships or jobs with joy and excellence somehow signifies that they're accepting their sorry state of affairs. They reason that their bad attitude and unhappiness will somehow moti-vate them to leave. This type of mindset is rarely successful, and usually it ends up eating away at your sense of self. It's simply wrong-headed to think that sacrificing noble values for ignoble ones will propel you to greater heights.

In every moment of every day, you have the power to be-come a more substantial person. When the clerk at the store gives you too much change, you can choose to return it. When someone wants to tell you a racist joke, you can choose to let that person know that you would rather not hear it. When a friend wants to spread a vicious rumor, you can choose to excuse yourself from the conversation. When your spouse or child acts out, you can choose to control your anger and move toward understanding what these actions are trying to tell you. Whether you're a vice president of a major corporation or an entry-level clerk at a department store, whether you're looking for love or committed to a loving relationship, when you look over the menu of your life, you can say, "I'll choose excellence!"

take a moment...

1. Identify three "whines" that you engage in.

2. Describe three possible solutions to the above "whines."

3. What fears are preventing you from following through on these solutions?

4. Can you identify personal values that are important to you?

5. Describe a scenario from your past when you lost your psychological balance because of external circumstances. Now write down how the scenario would have been different if you had stuck to your internal values instead of reacting to intense emotions.

Resistance
is futile

This book has examined the concept of your fears and insecurities and how you resist becoming conscious of them. Challenging the state of your life—demanding something more, something healthy and self-affirming—requires resolute intention and herculean courage. Elaborate defenses, and your difficulty in becoming conscious of what they're defending against, create a psychological dynamic that hinders this. Think for a moment how different civilization would be if these fear-based psychological defenses weren't in play. Imagine what could be accomplished! Unfortunately, insecurities, self-loathing, and the fear of failure, along with all the psychological defenses that were created to keep them out of conscious view, are fundamental to our human experience. This is why we struggle.

This dynamic can be in revealed in the story of Darren, a man who experiences more than his share of tragedy. Darren's a happy-go-lucky guy—young, handsome, healthy, and intelligent. He has the world at his feet, and the future looks bright indeed. One day, he's working out at the gym when his little finger gets caught in a weight machine and is ripped completely from his hand. It's so badly mangled that the doctors can't reattach it. Darren's distraught. A guitar player and athletically active, he's convinced that his life is ruined. He's always been very conscious of his appearance, and he thinks that people will be put off by his deformity. Day after day, he curses his bad luck: "It's so unfair! I can't believe this happened! Oh, how I wish I could go back in time and redo that day!"

Darren's woefulness goes on for a few weeks until, feeling a little better, he plans a barbecue for some friends. While he's putting meat in the food processor, he slips, and the same hand that's already lost a finger goes directly into the spinning blades and gets completely ground up! "Oh my God!" he exclaims. "What am I going to do now? There's no way that I can play guitar! What about golf? People will talk about me behind my back when they see me! Women aren't going to want to be with me! My life's ruined! I'd gladly accept my finger being gone if only I could have my hand back!"

Darren's devastated. He sits around week after week lamenting his streak of horrible luck. Who would ever have guessed that one person could be so cursed? A few later, he's walking past a construction site when suddenly a table-saw blade comes loose, flies two hundred feet through the air, and slices off his already maimed arm! When he wakes up in the hospital, he's inconsolable: "How could this have happened? My entire arm! Losing my finger was horrible—losing my hand was even worse! Now my entire arm is gone! At least when I had my arm I could look somewhat normal and could maneuver myself around. Now what am I supposed to do? I'd gladly accept losing my finger *and* my hand if only I can get the rest of my arm back! Please, please . . . I want my arm back so badly!"

By now I'm sure you've heard enough about slicing and dicing and can guess the point of this story. It speaks to the old saying: "I used to complain because I had no shoes until I met a man who had no feet." Perhaps the only way that Darren could truly appreciate what he had was to lose it. In *The Wizard of Oz*, Dorothy was convinced that nothing could be worse than the chores and humdrum life of a farm girl. Through her adventures "over the rainbow," she came to realize how good she actually had it. In the same vein, this idea—that it's only through losing things that we can truly appreciate them—may be informative in understanding your psychological evolution.

Someone can explain to you in intricate detail what an orange tastes like, but you'll never really know how one tastes for sure until you actually put one in your mouth. You can't really understand what it's like to be old until you see the lines when you look at yourself in the mirror or until waiters start to call you "sir" or "madam." You can't truly understand what it's like to have a loved one die until you receive a phone call in the middle of the night. You may have thought that making your first million was all important, but when you find out that the spouse you've loved and cherished is having an affair or is filing for divorce because you're never home, you instantly (albeit too late) gain perspective. These types of struggles—the small ones but especially the big ones—and the consequences they leave in their wake force you to evolve.

All destruction brings with it an element of the constructive. Volcanoes darken skies and submerge cities under rivers of molten lava, but they're also primary forces in the creation of islands and new land. Stars and galaxies collide with unfathomable destruction, but those collisions are also responsible for the creation of millions of new stars. Fires decimate entire forests, but they also clear space, burn away tree canopies so sunlight can reach the ground, and create fertilizer from the ashes of the burned trees, all of which leads to spectacular new growth. And on the human level, the challenges that you're forced to face often cause havoc, but they can also serve as a reminder that you must strive for something better.

You need to listen to the cries from deep within. This is what brought you to this book. You want to squeeze out every last ounce of passion, intelligence, creativity, integrity, joy, and self-actualization from this life. Don't make your life goal one of being liked, being accepted, or living without confrontation. While these can all be terrific things to have as *part* of your life, you don't want to lead with them. Instead, you want to lead with a desire for passion, creativity, imagination, and the realization of your dreams. You want to lay claim to the person you truly are—and, in the process, all of these other aspects will follow.

Commit to moving past your role as personal commentator: "I should go back to school," "I know I should lose weight," "One of these days I'll tell my father that I'm angry because he never had any time for me," "I'll open my restaurant when the time is right." Instead of reveling in your potential, commit to shutting your mouth, getting up off your behind, and *taking specific action!*

Personal evolution entails asking "Why?" and then having the courage to *live* differently once you find the answer. Engaging in this battle is like taking on the role of the hero in a super-suspense movie. Every door you open is fraught with danger where you're likely to find horrible feelings (that you're stupid, bad, worthless) and realities (that your parents didn't really care about you, that your father was competitive, that your mother was jealous) that bring you pain in the moment but growth and self-actualization eventually.

> *If you can face uncomfortable feelings instead of hiding from them, you will find that accepting these feelings will lead to peace and psychological freedom.*

Your defenses are like double agents—they pretend to be your friends by telling you that you're not at fault for your missteps and by giving you small victories (a job that isn't horrible, a relationship that's tolerable). But all the while they're (unwittingly) working against your quest for self-actualization. They're encouraging you to settle. You'll medicate yourself by watching television and movies that allow you to live vicariously through the actualized lives of virtual people. You may use a narrow view of religion or spirituality as a substitute for achieving self-actualization. Why challenge yourself to move past a psychologically comfortable (but depressing and unfulfilling) life if heaven or paradise lies just a few years away? Following this idea, it may make sense to take your foot off the gas, coast, be "nice," and wait for your ultimate reward.

I believe that our true nature is to constantly grow and evolve psychologically. I believe that psychological evolution is a core drive. Perfection—be it perfect love, knowledge, passion, or creativity—is "perfect" only *in* that moment and *for* that moment. This means that when seemingly "perfect" love has been achieved, it can and should become deeper; that seemingly "perfect" knowledge will become greater; that seemingly "perfect" passion will become more intense, and that "perfect" creativity will become more inspired.

I believe that your entire psychology is structurally set up as a way for you to strive to continually reinvent what's "perfect" in the moment. Your personal unconscious may be a representation of a much larger unconscious/consciousness because the goal, from both a personal and perhaps universal and even spiritual perspective, may be to make the unconscious conscious. All of life—all of creation—is really constant evolution in its purest and most awesome form. The ending is just the beginning of what's next. Growth is hardwired. At every step in the process, you're poised to make the next step in your quest for self-actualization. All that's required is your intention and your action. Resistance is futile. The future is now. Take this step, and the title of your new book will be:

"Finally, My Life Has Come to This!"

Epilogue

Someone once asked Einstein how he would go about solving a problem if he was given only one hour. He said: "If I had an hour to solve a problem, I'd spend fifty-five minutes thinking about the problem and five minutes thinking about solutions."

When you're uncomfortable, you want to fix the problem instantly. This tendency is especially prevalent in today's age of instant gratification. You have so many options available that promise to make you feel good. The trick is not just to feel good. It's to feel complete, whole, integrated, and actualized—something much more profound and difficult to achieve than just feeling "good."

Perhaps, like Einstein, you need to do more "being" and less "quick-fixing." You are, after all, a Human *Being!*

At the beginning of this book, I asked you to make it your own. I'm certain that each one of you has had your own experiences that helped create the many defenses that have exerted and continue to exert their influence on you. As I've repeatedly stated throughout this book, your defenses were not created to hurt you. On the contrary, their sole purpose is to protect you from harm. Listen to them. Listen to what all your fears, irrational thoughts, and dysfunctional behaviors are telling you. You weren't born a loser, fat, drunk, or depressed. These are symptoms of emotional and psychological traumas. Listen to what's underneath these issues. I know it's hard. It's so hard that you'll be tempted to accept the status quo, as miserable as it may be, rather than venturing out into the scary unknown.

Following the concepts outlined in this book requires a great deal of courage because when you make the effort to embrace excellence, things usually get worse before they get better. You need to be courageous and patient because the rewards that come with facing your most devastating psychological secrets are usually ambiguous and distant.

Courage is required, but so is faith. You'll make this journey with no guarantee of success. Only you can determine whether or not you have enough faith and courage to see your way through. Psychological health and all that goes with it is available to you, but you have to want it more than you want the comforts that go along with remaining oblivious. But, armed with the courage of a psychological warrior and the faith of a true believer, a life of passion, fulfillment and joy is waiting for you.

What an adventure! The pot of gold awaits! What a journey you are on!

Acknowledgments

There are many people who deserve thanks and gratitude for their help and support. Debbie, Bruce, Andrew, Kelly, John, Drew, Mary, Melinda, Toby, and Michelle were exceptionally insightful and instrumental in leading me to places that I was unable to see. My family and friends have put up with my idiosyncrasies while always believing and supporting me. They are my backbone and comfort.

I also want to acknowledge the numerous individuals who have trusted me to be part of their lives and their growth. This book could not have been written without their trust and courage. The joy of my work is that as I help others with their personal growth, there's a parallel process in which I'm allowed to explore myself and experience my own as well. I feel honored and deeply thankful to be allowed to accompany them on their journey.

About the Author

Gary Penn, PhD, is a licensed psychologist with an established practice in Brentwood, California. His clientele includes top business executives from the entertainment, sports, and professional worlds, as well as a wide variety of adults and couples.

His mission is to help people to break free from their damaged psychology—to work with people who are struggling to find clarity, happiness, meaning, and purpose in their lives . . . people who are struggling with lives that are not being fully lived . . . people whose insecurities, fears, and damaged personal, social, and communication skills are preventing them from evolving psychologically.

In addition to his clinical practice, Dr. Penn conducts personal growth seminars as well as leadership and conflict resolution seminars for individuals, couples, and corporations. He is a prolific writer who has written articles that have appeared in numerous national magazines. In addition, he has been featured in such publications as *Time* magazine, *The New York Times*, *USA Today*, and the *Los Angeles Times*. He has also appeared on "Leesa" and "Good Morning America," among other television programs. Earlier in his career, Dr. Penn was a talk-show host on KFI Radio, one of the top-rated talk stations in the nation.

Dr. Penn is also an adjunct professor of psychology at Antioch University and California Graduate Institute.

He can be contacted through his website:

www.DrGaryPenn.com

CPSIA information can be obtained at www.ICGtesting.com
Printed in the USA
BVOW011007180313

315797BV00024B/1312/P